SO-APP-383

MICROSOFT® OFFICE 2000 QUICK REFERENCE

Nancy Warner

201 West 103rd Street, Indianapolis, Indiana 46290

MICROSOFT OFFICE® 2000 QUICK REFERENCE

ISBN: 0-7897-1932-0

International ISBN: 0-7897-2090-6

Library of Congress Catalog Card Number: 98-88238

Printed in the United States of America

First Printing: May 1999

01   00   99   4   3   2   1

TRADEMARKS

WARNING AND DISCLAIMER

Executive Editor Jim Minatel	**Managing Editor** Thomas F. Hayes	**Proofreader** Tricia Sterling
Author Nancy Warner	**Project Editor** Karen S. Shields	**Interior Designer** Louisa Klucznik
Development Editor Susan Hobbs	**Copy Editor** Julie McNamee	**Cover Designer** Dan Armstrong
Technical Editor Scott Warner	**Indexer** Becky Hornyak	**Layout Technician** Steve Balle-Gifford

PART 1

OFFICE QUICK REFERENCE

DETECT AND REPAIR

Detect and repair automatically finds and fixes errors in the Office applications you are currently running. Close any other applications you have open and have your installation disks nearby.

Run Detect and Repair

1. Choose **Help, Detect and Repair** in the Office application with which you are having trouble.
2. Click the [Start] button in the Detect and Repair dialog box. Note that clicking the **Restore My Shortcuts While Repairing** check box adds the program shortcuts to the Windows Start menu.
3. Select the application(s) you want to **Cancel, Retry,** or **Ignore**.

See Also Help, Office Assistant, Office on the Web

DIALOG BOXES

Windows uses dialog boxes to display information to, and request input from, the end user. The different ways you can provide input are through buttons, text boxes, option buttons, check boxes, spin boxes, list boxes, and drop-down list boxes.

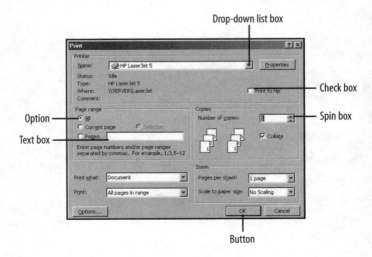

Get Help in a Dialog Box

1. Click the [?] in the upper-right area of the title bar.
2. Click the item you need help with and a ScreenTip appears with descriptive information. Click anywhere on your desktop or press the **Esc** key to continue.

Close a Dialog Box

Click the **Close** [X] button in the upper-right corner on the title bar or press the **Esc** key. If it happens to be a dialog box where you can apply changes and still exit the dialog box, you can also click the [Cancel] or [Close] button to close.

See Also Menus, What's This?

DOCKED TOOLBARS
see Toolbars   pg 251

EXIT APPLICATIONS

When you no longer want to work in an application, exit the application and return to the Windows desktop.

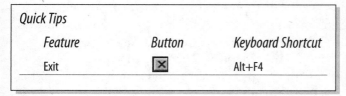

Quick Tips		
Feature	*Button*	*Keyboard Shortcut*
Exit	[X]	Alt+F4

Exit an Application

1. Click the **Close** [X] button in the upper-right corner of the application window. You are asked whether you want to save your work.
2. Click the [No] button to close and lose any unsaved changes, or the [Yes] button to save your work (refer to **Save** if you have problems saving your work). Click the [Cancel] button to return to working in the document.

See Also Start Applications

FAX

Faxing a document is as easy as printing a document. Keep in mind that you must have fax software installed on your computer and an outgoing phone line.

Send an Office Document As a Fax

1. Choose **File**, **Print** to open the Print dialog box.
2. Select **Microsoft Fax** from the **Printer Name** dropdown list.
3. Click the OK button to send the fax. Depending on your fax software, enter the phone number to which you want to fax and a fax cover letter if necessary.

See Also Help

FLOATING TOOLBARS
see Toolbars   pg 251

HELP

You can get help in Office 2000 in a couple of different ways. The Help Contents is similar to using the table of contents in a book. The Answer Wizard behaves similar to the Office Assistant in which you ask questions and it searches for related topics. The Help Index lets you type the word or phrase you want to find and then view a list of all matching topics.

Quick Tips		
Feature	**Button**	**Keyboard Shortcut**
Help	?	F1

Get Contents Help

1. Press the **F1** key and then click the **Contents** tab.
2. Click the **+** (plus sign) of a topic to list all the subtopics. Click a subtopic to see the information displayed in the description area.

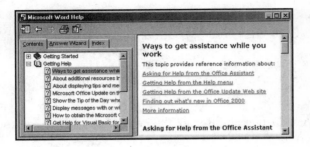

3. Click the **Close** ☒ button to exit Help.

Get Answer Wizard Help

1. Press the **F1** key and click the **Answer Wizard** tab.

2. Type in your question.

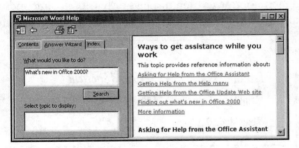

3. Click the ⌊ Search ⌋ button and select a topic to display.

4. Click the **Close** ☒ button to exit Help.

Get Index Help

1. Press the **F1** key and click the **Index** tab.

2. Type in a keyword and click the ⌊ Search ⌋ button.

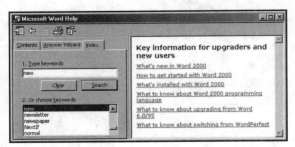

3. Select the topic you want in the description area.
4. Click the **Close** ☒ button to exit Help.

Print Help Topics

1. Select the Help item you want to print.
2. Click the 🖨 button on the toolbar.

See Also Detect and Repair, Office Assistant, Office on the Web, What's This?

MENUS

The menu bar is just below the title bar and varies from application to application. You select commands on the menu to perform operations. Office 2000 now has a *personalized* menu option, which displays only those commands relevant to what you are doing in the application at that time.

Quick Tips	
Feature	*Keyboard Shortcut*
Menu Mode On	F10
Menu Mode On	Alt

Use Personalized Menus

1. Click the menu command that you want to open.
2. Click the [⊻] to show all the commands available.

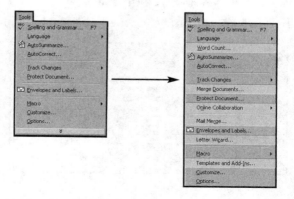

3. Click the command on the menu you want and the menu closes automatically.

Use Regular Menus

1. Click the menu command that you want to open.

2. Click the command on the menu you want and the menu closes automatically.

Close a Menu Without Choosing a Command

1. Click the menu command that you want to open.

2. Click elsewhere on the desktop or press the **Esc**, **Alt**, or **F10** keys to close the menu.

Turn Personalized Menus On/Off

1. Choose **Tools, Customize** and click the **Options** tab.

2. Select the **Menus Show Recently Used Commands First** option if you want to turn the personalized menus on. Deselect the option to turn them off.

3. Click the [Close] button to accept changes and return to the application.

See Also Dialog Boxes, Toolbars

OFFICE ASSISTANT

The Office Assistant is a quick way to search for help on a particular topic and find shortcuts in Office applications. It helps you find instructions and tips for getting your work done more easily.

Quick Tips		
Feature	*Button*	*Keyboard Shortcut*
Help	🔲	F1

Show and Hide the Office Assistant

1. Choose **Help, Show the Office Assistant**.

2. Choose **Help, Hide the Office Assistant**.

Ask the Office Assistant Questions

1. Click the **Assistant** character if it is onscreen; otherwise, click the 🔁 button on the Standard toolbar.

2. Type in the question or term for which you want information and click the ▭ Search ▭ button.

3. Click the bullet next to the information you want and select the topic you want Microsoft Office to reference.

4. Click the **Close** ▭✕▭ button in the upper-right corner of the Help window to close it.

Changing the Assistant

1. Right-click the **Assistant** and click **Choose Assistant** from the shortcut menu.

2. Peruse your options using the ▭ Next > ▭ and ▭ <Back ▭ buttons in the Gallery page of the Office Assistant dialog box.

3. Click the ▭ OK ▭ button when you finish selecting an Assistant.

Turn the Assistant Off

1. Right-click the **Assistant** and click **Options** from the shortcut menu.

2. Select the **Use the Office Assistant** option and click the ▭ OK ▭ button.

See Also Detect and Repair, Help, Office on the Web, What's This?

OFFICE ON THE WEB

Microsoft Office on the Web takes you to the Microsoft Office Web site and provides access to download free stuff, product news, frequently asked questions, online support, and much more information.

Microsoft Office Update Web Site

1. Choose **Help, Office on the Web**.

2. Peruse the Microsoft Office Web Site with your Web browser.

---

3. Click the **Close** ☒ button when you want to return to the Office application.

See Also Detect and Repair, Help, Office Assistant, What's This?

PROGRAM
see Macros   pg 243

PROPERTIES

Details about a file that help identify it—author's name, document title, topic, keywords—are known as *file properties*. Use file properties to help organize your files or display file information.

Add Document Summary Information

1. Choose **File**, **Properties** and click the **Summary** tab.
2. Type the information about your document that you want to save.
3. Click the ☐ OK ☐ button to return to the application.

QUIT
see Exit Application   pg 3

RIGHT MOUSE BUTTON

When you right-click an item in your workspace, a shortcut menu appears (also known as a pop-up or context menu). Shortcut menus include the commands you use most for whatever is currently selected.

Use a Shortcut Menu

1. Right-click an object or some text.
2. Click a command on the shortcut menu that appears; the menu automatically goes away and the command is performed.

TIP

To leave a shortcut menu without making a selection, press the Esc key or left-click elsewhere on the desktop.

See Also Menus

SCREENTIPS

see Toolbars   pg 251

SHORTCUT BAR

The shortcut bar enables you to open applications, create new Office documents, open Office documents, and perform Office tasks at the click of a button, instead of using the Start menu.

Activate the Shortcut Bar

1. Choose **Start**, **Programs**, **Office Tools**, **Microsoft Office Shortcut Bar**.

2. Click the **No** button if you want to review the shortcut bar; click the **Yes** button if you want the shortcut bar to start automatically when you start Windows.

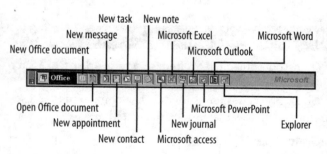

Use the Shortcut Bar

1. Move the mouse pointer over the Office shortcut bar buttons to view the ScreenTips.

2. Click an Office shortcut bar button to perform a particular action.

See Also Start Applications, Toolbars

START APPLICATIONS

When an application is installed, a copy of the application
icon is placed in the Programs menu by default. From this
menu, you can launch the applications you have installed.
If an application doesn't show up in your Programs menu,
it probably wasn't installed.

Use the Start Button

1. Click the **🔲Start** button in the taskbar to open the
   Start menu.
2. Click the **Programs** command to open the **Programs**
   menu.
3. Click the application you want to start.

Create and Use a Shortcut Icon

1. Locate the folder or file (even an application's exe-
   cutable file, .exe) in Windows Explorer. Click the folder
   or file and drag and drop it at the new location.
2. Select **Create Shortcut(s) Here** from the pop-up menu
   that appears; the shortcut is created.
3. Double-click the shortcut icon to launch the application.

See Also Exit Applications, Shortcut Bar, Switch Between
Documents and Applications

SWITCH BETWEEN DOCUMENTS AND APPLICATIONS

You can have multiple Office applications and documents
open at a time and switch between them whenever you
want. You can use the Windows taskbar to move quickly
from one open application window or Office document to
another.

> Quick Tips
>
> | Feature | Keyboard Shortcut |
> |---|---|
> | Switch Between Documents and Applications | Alt+Tab |

Switch Between Documents and Applications

1. Click the taskbar button for the document you want to use.
2. Click the taskbar button for a different Office application.

See Also Shortcut Bar, Start Applications

TOOLBARS

To perform tasks, you can click a toolbar button with your mouse pointer. Doing so is faster than using a menu command, especially for frequent or repetitive tasks. The Standard toolbar contains buttons for the most common commands. The Formatting toolbar contains lists and buttons for the most common formatting commands.

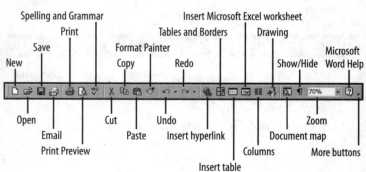

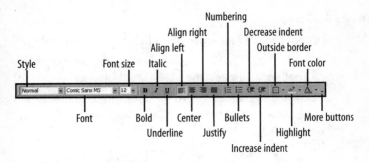

Float and Dock a Toolbar

1. Press and hold down the left mouse button on the vertical bar on the leftmost side of the toolbar. Then drag and drop the toolbar onto your desktop so that it looks like it is floating.

2. Click the toolbar title and drag it to a different edge on the desktop so that it looks like it is docked.

3. Double-click the title portion of the toolbar and the toolbar automatically returns to its previous location.

Show and Hide Toolbars

1. Choose **View, Toolbars,** and select the toolbar you want to show. Toolbars that are displayed have a check next to their name in the menu.

2. Choose **View, Toolbars,** and deselect the toolbar you want to hide. The check in the menu and the toolbar onscreen will disappear.

Add or Remove Buttons

1. Click the **More** button and select **Add or Remove Buttons**.

2. Check a particular command button to add it to the toolbar; uncheck a command button to remove it from the toolbar.

Create a New Toolbar

1. Choose **Tools, Customize** and click the **Toolbar** tab.
2. Click the [New...] button, type in the name of the new toolbar, and click the [OK] button.
3. Click the **Commands** tab in the Customize dialog box and select a button from the **Categories** and **Commands** list boxes.

4. Click and drag the command to the location you want and drop it onto a toolbar.
5. Click the [Close] button on the Customize dialog box.

Modify a Toolbar Command Button

1. Choose **Tools, Customize** and click the **Commands** tab.
2. Click the command button on the toolbar you want to modify; the button appears with a black line around it. Choose **Modify Selection, Change Button Image**, and select an image.
3. Click the [Modify Selection ▾] button and choose **Default Style**, which displays only the button image.
4. Click the [Close] button on the Customize dialog box.

See Also Menus, Shortcut Bar

TROUBLESHOOT
see Detect and Repair   pg 2

WHAT'S THIS? HELP

A ScreenTip of a command gives you concise information about the command's function. What's This? Help offers a more thorough explanation of what a command does.

Quick Tips

Feature	*Keyboard Shortcut*
What's This?	Shift+F1

Use What's This?

1. Choose **Help, What's This?** and the mouse pointer becomes a question mark pointer.
2. Click the command or object you want explained and read the What's This? pop-up.
3. Click anywhere in your workspace, or press the **Esc,** **Alt,** or **F10** keys to clear the pop-up information.

See Also Detect and Repair, Help, Office Assistant, Office on the Web

V
W
X

PART 2

WORD QUICK REFERENCE

ACCEPT OR REJECT CHANGES

When you are ready to finalize tracked changes in a document, you determine which changes to accept and which to reject.

> *Quick Tips*
>
> | *Feature* | *Button* | *Keyboard Shortcut* |
> |---|---|---|
> | Revision Marks Toggle | TRK | Ctrl + ⬆Shift + E |

Review Revision Marks

1. Right-click **Track Changes** TRK on the status bar and choose **Accept or Reject Changes** from the shortcut menu.

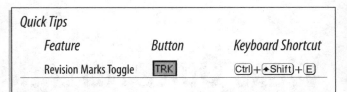

Accept all changes in the document. Undo the previous item you accepted or rejected.

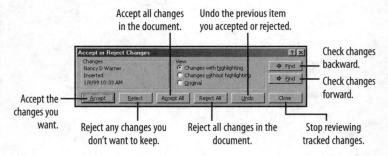

Check changes backward.
Check changes forward.

Accept the changes you want.
Reject any changes you don't want to keep.
Reject all changes in the document.
Stop reviewing tracked changes.

2. Click the ⇨ Find button and Word searches for, finds, and highlights the first (if any) occurrence of a tracked change. Word automatically takes you to the next tracked change after you accept or reject a selected change. If you don't want to accept or reject a particular tracked change, click one of the **Find** buttons to move to the next change. Click the OK button to continue checking from the beginning of the document (if you started anywhere but the beginning) or to acknowledge that Word found no other changes.

See Also Track Changes

ACTIVE DOCUMENT
see Workspace   pg 254

ALIGNMENT

When you enter text into a document, the text automatically aligns flush (even) with the left margin. However, you can change the alignment of text at any time, before or after you have entered the text.

Quick Tips		
Feature	*Button*	*Keyboard Shortcut*
Align Left	▤	Ctrl + L
Center	▤	Ctrl + E
Align Right	▤	Ctrl + R
Justify	▤	Ctrl + J

Align Existing Text

1. Select the text you want to align. Or, place the cursor somewhere in the paragraph you want to align.
2. Click the **Align Right** ▤ button on the Formatting toolbar to align right; the **Center** ▤ button to center text; the **Align Left** ▤ button to align left.

Align New Text

Click the appropriate alignment button on the Formatting toolbar and begin typing.

Click and Type

1. Choose **View, Print Layout**.
2. Double-click directly in the document where you want the text to begin and start typing.

See Also Indenting, Page Setup

AUTOCORRECT

Word 2000 lets you automatically correct yourself if you find you continue to make the same typing errors in your documents.

Replace Text As You Type

1. Choose **Tools, AutoCorrect; AutoCorrect** tab. Click the **Replace Text As You Type** check box.

2. Type the text you commonly spell wrong in the **Replace** text box. Type the correct text in the **With** text box.

3. Click the [Add] button to add or click the [Delete] button to delete an automatic correction. Click the [OK] button to accept your changes.

See Also Spelling and Grammar, Symbols

AUTOSUMMARIZE

This feature summarizes the main points in a document by analyzing sentences that contain frequently used words. These words determine which sentences make up the key points in your document.

Create a Document Summary

1. Choose **Tools, AutoSummarize** to open the AutoSummarize dialog box.

2. Select the **Type of Summary** and the **Length of Summary** from the **Percentage of Original** drop-down list.

3. Click the [OK] button. Word automatically highlights the important summary points and opens the AutoSummarize toolbar.

4. Click the **Highlight/Show Only Summary** [ ] button to toggle showing only the information in the summary. Click the [Close] button to cancel the summary.

See Also Word Count

BACKGROUND
see Web Pages   pg 253

BOLD
see Text   pg 250

BORDERS

You can add a border to any or all sides of a paragraph,
selected text, document, or object.

Add Text Borders

1. Select the text or place the cursor in your document
   where you want to add a border.
2. Click the **Borders** ▦ button on the Formatting toolbar
   and select the type of border you want to apply to the
   document from the drop-down list.

Format Borders

1. Place the cursor in the paragraph that contains a border.
2. Choose **Format, Borders and Shading; Borders** tab.
3. Select the optional **Setting, Style, Color,** and **Width**
   and click the **Preview** diagram to apply borders to particular sides of the selected paragraph. Click the
   OK button to accept changes and return to the
   document.

TIP

Choose the **Page Border** tab if you want to apply a border to
each document page.

See Also Shading

BREAKS

When a page is filled with text, Word automatically begins a new page by inserting a page break for you; however, there are times when you need to manually insert a page or section break.

Quick Tips	
Feature	*Keyboard Shortcut*
Page Break	Ctrl+⏎Enter

Create a Break

1. Choose **Insert, Break** to open the Break dialog box.

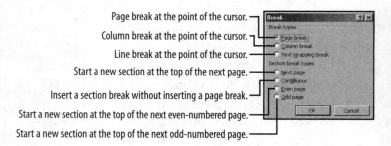

Page break at the point of the cursor.
Column break at the point of the cursor.
Line break at the point of the cursor.
Start a new section at the top of the next page.
Insert a section break without inserting a page break.
Start a new section at the top of the next even-numbered page.
Start a new section at the top of the next odd-numbered page.

2. Select the type of page break you want to insert in your document. Click the OK button to accept changes and return to the document.

TIP

To delete all types of breaks, place the cursor at the beginning of the break and press the Del key.

See Also Columns

BULLETED LISTS

Bulleted lists are useful for presenting a series of items when alpha or numeric order doesn't matter.

Quick Tips

Feature	Button	Keyboard Shortcut
Apply List Bullet		Ctrl+⬆Shift+L

Bullet Existing Text

1. Select the text you want to bullet.
2. Click the **Bullets** button on the Formatting toolbar. Notice that a bullet is added to each paragraph, not each sentence.

Bullet New Text

1. Click the **Bullets** button on the Formatting toolbar and begin typing.
2. Click the **Bullets** button again when you no longer want bullets.

Alter Bullets

1. Select the bulleted text you want to alter.
2. Choose **Format, Bullets and Numbering; Bulleted** tab.
3. Double-click the style of bullets you want to display.

See Also Numbered Lists

CASE CHANGE

Word allows you to easily change the case of text after it is written.

Quick Tips	
Feature	*Keyboard Shortcut*
Change Case	(◆Shift)+(F3)
Small Caps	(Ctrl)+(◆Shift)+(K)
All Caps	(Ctrl)+(◆Shift)+(A)

Change Case

1. Select the text you want to change.

2. Choose **Format**, **Change Case** to open the Change Case dialog box.

3. Select from the various capitalization options. Click the ⟨ OK ⟩ button to accept changes and return to the document.

See Also Fonts, Text

CENTER
see Alignment   pg 231

CHARACTER SPACING

The space above, below, before, and after characters can all be altered. This is convenient when you need a word or group of words to fit into a particular area.

Alter Character Spacing

1. Select the text where you want to alter the character spacing (or the entire document with Ctrl + A).

2. Choose **Format, Font; Character Spacing** tab.

Stretch or compress the text as a percentage of its current size horizontally.

Expand or condense the spacing between characters.

Raise or lower the text in relation to the baseline.

Automatically adjust the amount of space between character combinations.

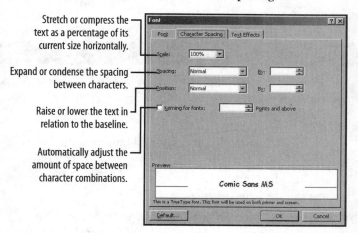

3. Select from the various character spacing options. Click the ⬚ OK ⬚ button to accept changes and return to the document.

See Also Fonts, Line Spacing, Paragraph Spacing, Symbols, Text

CHARTS

Word enables you to create and add charts to your documents without inserting an Excel worksheet. For more detailed information on charts, see Charts in the Excel section.

Insert Chart

1. Choose **Insert, Picture, Chart** to open a generic Excel datasheet and default 3D column chart.

2. Type the desired data into the datasheet and the chart updates automatically. Click directly in the document to hide the datasheet.

TIP

To edit the charted data, double-click directly on the chart and type your changes into the datasheet that appears.

See Also Excel Worksheets

CLIP ART

Clip art adds visual interest to your Word documents. You can choose from numerous professionally prepared images.

Insert Clip Art

1. Choose **Insert, Picture, Clip Art** to open the Insert ClipArt dialog box.

2. Click the **Categories** of clip art in the **Pictures** tab and scroll through the options.

3. Click the piece of clip art and choose **Insert Clip** 🔀 from the pop-up menu, which will insert the clip art into your document. Click the **Close** ✖ button to close the Insert ClipArt dialog box.

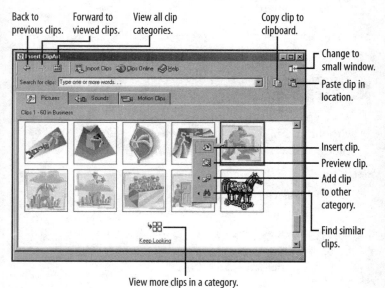

Back to previous clips.   Forward to viewed clips.   View all clip categories.   Copy clip to clipboard.

Change to small window.

Paste clip in location.

Insert clip.

Preview clip.

Add clip to other category.

Find similar clips.

View more clips in a category.

See Also Borders

CLIPBOARD
see Copy and Cut   pgs 235-236

CLOSE

When you finish working on a document, you can close it and continue to work on other documents. You can close a file with or without saving changes.

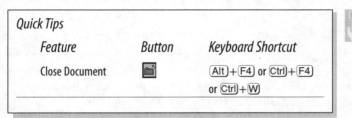

Quick Tips

Feature	Button	Keyboard Shortcut
Close Document		Alt + F4 or Ctrl + F4 or Ctrl + W

Close a Document

1. Click the **Close** ☒ button. If you made changes to the document, Word asks whether you want to save the changes.
2. Click the Yes button to save changes and close the document; click the No button to close the document without saving changes; click the Cancel button to return to working in your document without closing it or saving any changes.

See Also Save Documents

COLOR
see Fonts   pg 239

COLUMNS

You can display text in multiple columns on a page in a Word document. This is convenient when you want to create a brochure or newsletter or even differentiate between sections of a document.

Create Columns from Existing Text

1. Select the text you want to insert into columns.
2. Click the **Columns** ▦ button on the Standard toolbar and select the number of columns you want.

TIP

A column break must be added to move to the next column when entering text. See **Breaks** for more information.

Create New Columns

1. Click the **Columns** ▦ button on the Standard toolbar and select the number of columns you want.
2. Begin typing your text. Your text appears in columns until you insert a break.

Format Columns

1. Select the columnar text you want to format.
2. Choose **Format, Columns** to open the Columns dialog box.
3. Select the column **Presets** options and the **Number of Columns** from the spin box control. You can also manually alter the column **Width and Spacing** options. Click the OK button to accept changes and return to your document.

See Also Breaks, Tables

COMMENTS

When working in a document, you might find that you need to add a note in your document to remind you to verify some information when you work on the document later.

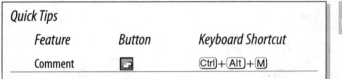

Quick Tips

Feature	Button	Keyboard Shortcut
Comment		Ctrl+Alt+M

Insert Comments

1. Select the text you want to comment on or place the cursor at the location where you want to insert a comment.
2. Choose **Insert**, **Comment** to open the Comment window.
3. Type your comment and click the Close button when finished. The commented text is highlighted and contains a comment number.
4. Move the mouse pointer over the highlighted comment indicator and the comment displays in a ScreenTip.

View All Comments

1. Choose **View**, **Comments** to open the Comments window.
2. Click the Close button when finished viewing.

Edit Comments

1. Select the highlighted comment, right-click the comment and choose **Edit Comment** from the shortcut menu.
2. Type the changes into the comment area and click the Close button to return to the document.

TIP

To delete a comment, select the highlighted comment, right-click it, and choose **Delete Comment** from the shortcut menu.

See Also Track Changes, Share and Protect Documents

COPY AND CUT

You can share information within and between documents in Word by copying and cutting text and objects. You can now copy/cut and paste up to 12 items onto the Clipboard at a time. The Clipboard is where items are stored before you paste them.

Quick Tips		
Feature	*Button*	*Keyboard Shortcut*
Copy		Ctrl + C or Ctrl + Insert
Copy Format		Ctrl + Shift + C
Copy Text Only		Shift + F2
Cut	✂	Ctrl + X or Shift + Del

Copy

1. Select the text or object you want to copy.
2. Click the **Copy** 📋 button on the Standard toolbar. The original text remains in this location and a copy is placed on the Clipboard ready to be pasted.

Cut

1. Select the text or object you want to cut.
2. Click the **Cut** ✂ button on the Standard toolbar. This removes the text from the location and places it on the Clipboard ready to be pasted.

Copy Multiple Items

1. Choose **View**, **Toolbars**, **Clipboard** to open the Clipboard toolbar.
2. Select an item you want to copy and click the **Copy** 📋 button on the Clipboard toolbar after each time you select an item (up to 12 items). You can also use the original **Copy** 📋 and **Cut** ✂ buttons on the Standard toolbar to place items on the Clipboard toolbar.

Copy an item to the Clipboard.   Paste all items in the document.

Paste an item into the document. ————————

Delete all items
from the Clipboard.

3. Move the mouse pointer over the Clipboard items and a
   ScreenTip displays what is contained in each copied clip
   (unless the clip is extensive, then only part of it appears).
   Click the clip to paste the item in the document.

TIP

The Clipboard toolbar automatically appears when you click the
Copy 🔳 or **Cut** 🔳 button multiple times. Click the **Close** 🔳
button to close the Clipboard toolbar, or choose **View, Toolbars,
Clipboard** to toggle the toolbar closed.

See Also Format Painter, Move Text, Objects, Paste

DOCUMENT MAP

Word automatically creates a Document Map when you use
built-in heading styles (Heading 1 through Heading 9) and
outline-level paragraphs (Level 1 through Level 9).

Use the Document Map

1. Click the **Document Map** 🔳 button to toggle between
   displaying the Document Map and your current document view.

2. Click a header in the Document Map to immediately
   view the information within the header.

See Also Styles, Views

DRAWING TOOLS

Word provides many tools for you to draw and format
shapes and text boxes in your document. These tools help
you add interest, information, and references to your documents.

D
E
F

Draw Shapes

1. Click the **Drawing** 🔟 button on the Standard toolbar to open the Drawing toolbar.
2. Select the shape you want to draw in your document: **Line** �, **Arrow** ◥, **Rectangle** ▢, or **Oval** ◯.
3. Click in the document and drag the crosshatch pointer to the desired shape size.

Add Shape Color

1. Click the shape you want to color in your document.
2. Click the appropriate button on the Drawing toolbar to select how you want to apply the color: **Fill Color** 🎨 and **Line Color** ✏. Click the desired color.

Alter Shape Style

1. Click the shape you want to style in your document.
2. Click the appropriate button on the Drawing toolbar to select how you want to apply the style: **Line Style** ▤, **Dash Style** ▦, **Arrow Style** 固, **Shadow** ◪, and **3D** ◩. Choose the desired style.

Insert AutoShapes

1. Click the AutoShapes ▾ button on the Drawing toolbar and select the particular shape you want to add to your document from the submenus.
2. Click in the document and drag the crosshatch pointer to the desired shape size.

Rotate Shapes

1. Click the shape you want to rotate in your document.
2. Click the **Free Rotate** ⟳ button on the Drawing toolbar.
3. Click the rotate pointer on the object rotate handles and drag the object to the desired rotation.

Add a Text Box

1. Click the **Text Box** ▣ button on the Drawing toolbar; or choose **Insert, Text Box**.

2. Click in the document and drag the crosshatch pointer to the desired shape size.

3. Click the **Font Control** ▣ button and select the font color; then type the information you want in the text box.

Add WordArt

1. Click the **WordArt** ◢ button on the Drawing toolbar.

2. Double-click a WordArt style in the WordArt Gallery dialog box and type the text in the Edit WordArt Text dialog box. Click the [OK] button to accept changes and return to the document.

See Also Clip Art, Objects

EMAIL

You can send the contents of a Word document as the substance of the email message. Refer to the **Outlook** section for more information on email.

Send a Document As an Email

1. Click the **Mail Recipient** ▣ button on the Standard toolbar.

2. Type the **To, Cc**, any changes to the **Subject** line (should be the filename), and any other changes in the document. Click the [Send a Copy] button and the email is sent.

Send a Document As an Email Attachment

1. Choose **File, Send To, Mail Recipient (As Attachment)**. This opens an email message and inserts the current document as an attachment.

2. Type the **To, Cc**, any changes to the **Subject** line (should be the filename), and any other changes in the document. Click the `⌐ Send ▾` button and the email is sent.

See Also Web Pages

ENVELOPES

You can create a single envelope with delivery and return address information without using the mail merge feature. For information on creating multiple envelopes, see **Mail Merge**.

Create Envelopes

1. Choose **Tools, Envelopes and Labels; Envelopes** tab.

2. Type in the **Delivery Address** and the **Return Address**. Then, click the `Options...` button to open the **Envelope Options** tab. Alter the **Envelope Size** and the address fonts. In addition, you can check the **Delivery Point Barcode** option. This prints the POSTNET bar code in a machine-readable representation of the zip code and delivery address, which helps your envelope reach its destination faster.

3. Click the **Printing Options** tab and select the **Feed Method** you want to use with your printer. Click the `OK` button to accept your changes. Click the `Print` button to print the envelope.

See Also Labels, Mail Merge

ENDNOTE
see Footnotes   pg 239

EXCEL WORKSHEETS

If you don't want to create a Word table in your document, you can embed an Excel worksheet directly in your document.

Quick Tips

Feature	Keyboard Shortcut
Update Source	Ctrl + ⬆Shift + F7

D
E
F

Insert a New Embedded Excel Worksheet

1. Place the cursor in the document where you want to insert the worksheet.

2. Click the **Insert Excel Spreadsheet** 🖬 button on the Standard toolbar and select the desired number of rows and columns.

3. Type in the data when the worksheet appears in the document.

Edit an Embedded Worksheet

1. Double-click directly on the worksheet in your document.

2. Edit the data as necessary; you can even click and drag the worksheet to a larger or smaller size.

See Also Charts, Tables

FIND TEXT

You can use Word's Find feature to locate text, characters, paragraph formatting, and even special characters.

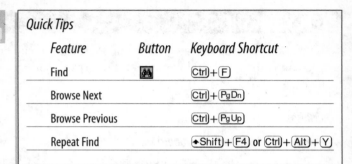

Quick Tips

Feature	Button	Keyboard Shortcut
Find		Ctrl + F
Browse Next		Ctrl + PgDn
Browse Previous		Ctrl + PgUp
Repeat Find		Shift + F4 or Ctrl + Alt + Y

Find Regular Text

1. Choose **Edit**, **Find** to open the Find and Replace dialog box.

2. Type the text you want to locate in the **Find What** list box.

3. Click the **Find Next** button to move to each occurrence within the document. If there aren't any to be found, Word notifies you that it has finished searching the document and that the item wasn't found.

Perform an Advanced Find

1. Choose **Edit**, **Find** and click the **More ∓** button to expand the **Search Options** in the Find and Replace dialog box.

2. Type the text you want to locate in the **Find What** list box.

3. Select from the various **Search** options.

- **Match Case**—For example, instead of finding all occurrences of lowercased **sales**, you can search specifically for initial-capped Sales.

- **Find Whole Words Only**—For example, **this** will find **the** instead of also finding **them** and **they**.

- **Use Wildcards**—For example, this will find character occurrences using the following *wildcards*: **? * [ ]**. **R?t** will find **rot** and **rat**; **r*t** will find **replenishment** and **rut**; **r[ao]t** will find **rot**, **rat**, and **root**.

- **Sounds Like**—For example, this will find phonetically similar text, such as **too**, **to**, **two**.

- **Find All Word Forms**—For example, this will find different word forms, such as **eat**, **ate**, **eaten**.

5. Select a specific **Format**, such as a particular Font or Special characters, such as a Section Break.

6. Click the [Find Next] button to move to each occurrence within the document. If there aren't any to be found, Word notifies you that it has finished searching the document and that the item wasn't found.

See Also Replace Text

FONTS

To draw attention to important words and phrases in a document, you can change the text font options.

Quick Tips

Feature	Button	Keyboard Shortcut
Font		Ctrl+Shift+F or Ctrl+D
Font Size		Ctrl+Shift+P
Grow Font		Ctrl+Shift+.
Grow Font One Point		Ctrl+]
Hidden Text		Ctrl+Shift+H
Shrink Font		Ctrl+Shift+,
Shrink Font One Point		Ctrl+[
Small Caps		Ctrl+Shift+K
Subscript	x_2	Ctrl+=
Superscript	x^2	Ctrl+Shift+=
Symbol Font		Ctrl+Shift+Q

Change Existing Text

1. Select the text in which you want to change the font.
2. Click the **Font** drop-down list box on the Formatting toolbar and select the desired font.
3. Click the **Font Size** drop-down list box on the Formatting toolbar and select the desired font size.
4. Click the **Font Color** drop-down list box on the Formatting toolbar and select the desired font color.

Set the Default Font

1. Choose **Format, Font; Font** tab.
2. Select the font you want to use as your default from the **Font** list box; then click the [Default...] button.
3. Click the [Yes] button in the message box to change the default font, which will affect all new documents in the Normal template. Click the [OK] button to accept changes and return to the document.

Add Font Effects to Text

1. Select the text to which you want to add a font effect.
2. Choose **Format, Font; Font** tab.

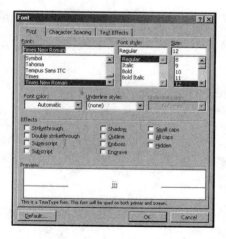

3. Select from the various types of **Effects**. Click the [OK] button to accept changes and return to the document.

See Also Text

FOOTNOTES AND ENDNOTES

Use a footnote at the end of a *page* to tell the reader the source of your information in a document. Use an endnote at the end of your *document* to cite research references.

Quick Tips	
Feature	*Keyboard Shortcut*
Footnote	Ctrl+Alt+F
Endnote	Ctrl+Alt+D

Insert Footnote or Endnote

1. Choose **View**, **Print Layout** view to see where you want the footnote or endnote inserted into your document. Click in the document where you want to insert the footnote or endnote number reference.

2. Choose **Insert**, **Footnote** to open the Footnote and Endnote dialog box.

3. Select the **Footnote** option to place the note at the end of the page, or the **Endnote** option to place the note at the end of the document. Click the ⏻ OK button to return to the document. If you are in Normal view, you are returned to the Footnotes or Endnotes window and must click the Close button to return to the document.

4. Type the text you want to appear in the footnote or endnote. Click anywhere in the document when finished.

> **TIP**
>
> Double-click the footnote or endnote reference to make any editing changes. To delete a footnote or endnote, select the reference in the text and press the Del key.

See Also Header and Footer, Comments, Views

FORMAT PAINTER

You can use the Format Painter to copy the format from a selected object or text and apply it to different objects or text you select.

Copy Character and Paragraph Formats

1. Select the text or object containing the format you want to copy and paste.

2. Click the **Format Painter** button on the Standard toolbar.

3. Select the text or object to which you want to apply the formatting; it formats automatically.

Copy Formats to Multiple Locations

1. Select the text or object containing the format you want to copy and paste. Double-click the **Format Painter** button on the Standard toolbar.

2. Select each particular text or object to automatically apply the formatting. Click the **Format Painter** button again when finished applying the format in multiple places.

See Also Copy and Cut, Paste

FRAMES
see Web Pages   pg 253

HEADER AND FOOTER

Headers and footers are text that prints at the top or bottom of every page in a document—headers at the top, footers at the bottom.

Insert Header and Footer

1. Choose **View, Header and Footer** to open the Header and Footer toolbar. Word automatically places the cursor in the Header area.

2. Type the text you want to print at the top of each page.

3. Click the **Switch Between Header and Footer** button on the Header and Footer toolbar to go from the header to the footer.

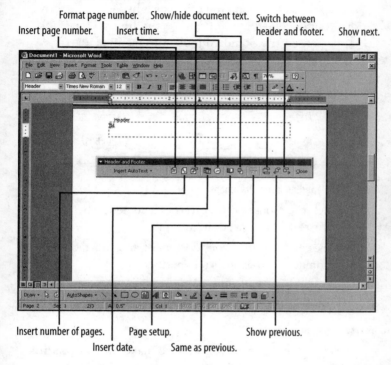

Format page number.   Show/hide document text.   Switch between

Insert page number.   Insert time.   header and footer.   Show next.

Insert number of pages.   Page setup.   Show previous.

Insert date.   Same as previous.

4. Double-click in the header or footer section to insert the cursor at a particular alignment and click any buttons on the toolbar to insert additional information. Click the Close button to return to the main document.

TIP

You can use the Tab⇄ key within the header and footer to alter the text alignment.

See Also Page Number, Page Setup, Print Preview, Views

HYPERLINKS

When you click a hyperlink, the document appears to *jump* to the related location. You can type a hyperlink directly into your document or you can use the **Insert Hyperlink** button on the Standard toolbar to manipulate the hyperlinks.

Quick Tips		
Feature	*Button*	*Keyboard Shortcut*
Hyperlink	🔗	Ctrl + K

Type a URL Hyperlink Into a Document

1. Click the mouse pointer in the document where you want to add the hyperlink.

2. Type the URL into your document and the address automatically becomes a hyperlink.

3. Move the mouse pointer over the hyperlink and the location displays in a ScreenTip.

Insert a Hyperlink

1. Select the text that you want to make into a hyperlink.

2. Click the **Hyperlink** 🔗 button on the Standard toolbar to open the Insert Hyperlink dialog box.

3. Type the link into the **Type the File or Web Page Name** text box or select from the **Recent Files**, **Browsed Pages**, or **Inserted Links** list. Click the OK button to accept changes and return to the document.

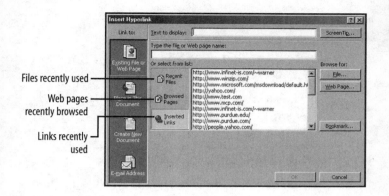

Files recently used —

Web pages recently browsed

Links recently used

TIP

To delete a hyperlink, right-click the hyperlink and choose **Hyperlink, Remove Hyperlink**. To edit a hyperlink, right-click the hyperlink and choose **Hyperlink, Edit Hyperlink**. Make the changes and click the OK button.

See Also Objects, Text, Save Documents, Web Pages

INDENTS

You can indent a line, paragraph, or multiple paragraphs in a document to the right of the left margin to make text stand out.

Quick Tips		
Feature	*Button*	*Keyboard Shortcut*
Increase Indent		Ctrl+M
Hanging Indent		Ctrl+T
Undo Indent		Ctrl+Shift+M
Undo Hang		Ctrl+Shift+T

Increase and Decrease an Indent

1. Select the text you want to indent.
2. Click the **Increase Indent** 📰 button to increase the text indent 1/2 inch at a time.
3. Click the **Decrease Indent** 📰 button to decrease the text indent 1/2 inch at a time.

Insert an Indent

1. Select the text you want to indent.
2. Click the horizontal ruler tab and indent settings button to choose the type of indent you want.

Click to toggle through indents and tabs.   Indents the first line of a paragraph to the right.   Indent the paragraph to the left.

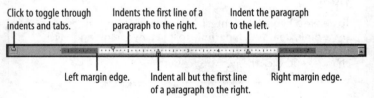

Left margin edge.   Indent all but the first line of a paragraph to the right.   Right margin edge.

3. Move the mouse pointer over the ruler where you want to place the indent, and click once directly on the ruler.

Remove an Indent

1. Click in the paragraph where you want to remove an indent.
2. Click the horizontal ruler indent marker and drag it flush with the left margin edge.

> **TIP**
>
> You can move an indent by clicking the indent indicator on the ruler and dragging it to the desired location on the ruler.

See Also Alignment, Page Setup, Tabs

ITALIC
see Text   pg 250

JUSTIFICATION
see Alignment   pg 231

LABELS

Word can help you create and print one label or multiple labels for a mass mailing.

Print Labels

1. Choose **Tools, Envelopes and Labels**; **Labels** tab.

2. Type the text you want on the label in the **Address** text box, or click the **Address Book** 📖 button to select from your address book.

3. Select whether you want a **Full Page of the Same Label** or a **Single Label**. Click the [Options...] button and select the **Label Products** and **Product Number**. Click the [OK] button to accept the changes.

4. Click the [Print] button in the Envelopes and Labels dialog box to send the labels to the printer.

See Also Envelopes, Mail Merge, Print

LANDSCAPE
see Page Setup   pg 245

LINE SPACING

Word enables you to set the amount of vertical space between lines of text.

Quick Tips

Feature	Button	Keyboard Shortcut
Line Spacing 1	▭	Ctrl + 1
Line Spacing 1.5	▤	Ctrl + 5
Line Spacing 2	▤	Ctrl + 2

Alter Line Spacing

1. Select the text where you want to alter the line spacing.

2. Choose **Format**, **Paragraphs**; **Indents and Spacing** tab.

3. Click the **Line Spacing** drop-down list box and select the size you want. Click the [OK] button to accept the changes and return to the document.

See Also Character Spacing, Fonts, Text

LINK OBJECTS
see Worksheets   pg 254

MACROS

You can create a macro that will accomplish just about any task. With the macro recording option, you can record your actions, and then these actions will be performed for you when you run the macro.

Quick Tips		
Feature	Button	Keyboard Shortcut
Macro	▶	Alt + F8

Create a Macro

1. Choose **Tools**, **Macro**, **Record New Macro** to open the Record Macro dialog box.

2. Type a name in the **Macro Name** text box.

3. Click the [OK] button. The Macro toolbar appears with the **Stop Recording** ■ and **Pause Recording** ▮▮ buttons.

4. Perform any tasks that you want the macro to record and click the **Stop Recording** ■ button when finished.

Run a Macro

1. Press the Alt+F8 keys to open the Macros dialog box.
2. Double-click the **Macro Name** and the macro runs.

TIP

To delete a macro, press Alt+F8 to open the Macro dialog box. Click the Macro name and click the ⬚⬚Delete⬚⬚ button; a dialog box appears and asks whether you want to delete the macro. Click the ⬚⬚Yes⬚⬚ button to delete the macro. Click the **Close** ✕ button to return to your document.

See Also Find Text, Replace Text

MAIL MERGE

Word enables you to create a document that merges a main document with a data source. You create the main document and the data source, insert the field names into the main document, and merge the documents.

Quick Tips

Feature	Keyboard Shortcut
Mail Merge Check	Alt+⬆Shift+K
Mail Merge Edit Data Source	Alt+⬆Shift+E
Mail Merge to Document	Alt+⬆Shift+N
Mail Merge to Printer	Alt+⬆Shift+M

Create the Main Document

1. Choose **Tools, Mail Merge** to open the Mail Merge Helper dialog box.
2. Click the ⬚⬚Create ▾⬚⬚ button and choose **Form Letters** from the drop-down list.
3. Click the ⬚⬚New Main Document⬚⬚ button to create a new main document.

4. Click the [Edit ▾] button and select the **Form Letter:** *document name.*

5. Type the document the way you want the form letter to appear, leaving blank spaces where you want the merged data entered. Notice the Mail Merge toolbar displays, which can help you when inserting field names into your form letter.

6. Choose **File, Save** to open the Save As dialog box. Assign a **File Name** and click the [🖫 Save] button to save the changes to your main document.

Get Data Source

1. Choose **Tools, Mail Merge** to open the Mail Merge Helper dialog box. You can also click the **Mail Merge** [🖼] button to open the dialog box at any time.

2. Click the [Get Data ▾] button, select an option from the drop-down list according to your data, and follow these steps:

   ■ **Create Data Source**—This opens the Create Data Source dialog box where you can add, remove, or change the order of your data source fields. Click the [OK] button to return to the mail Merge Helper dialog box. Type a name for your mailing list source data document and click [🖫 Save] in the Save As dialog box. Word informs you that the created data source is empty, so you need to click the [Edit Data Source] button to begin adding information to the data source fields in the Data Form dialog box (use the [Tab↹] key to move between fields). Click the [Add New] button each time you add data for a new entry. Click the [OK] button when finished.

   ■ **Open Data Source**—This opens the Open Data Source dialog box where you can select the document that contains the fields to use as your data source and click the [🖻 Open] button. Click the [Edit Main Document] button; view and add merge fields in your data source document, if no merged fields were found, and then save changes as necessary.

- **Use Address Book**—This opens the Use Address Book dialog box where you can select the address book to use to insert fields as a data source and click the [OK] button. Click the [Edit Main Document] button to view and edit the fields in your data source document, then save changes as necessary.

Insert Field Names

1. Place the cursor in the main document where you want to insert a merged field from the data source.

2. Click the [Insert Merge Field ▾] button on the Mail Merge toolbar and select from the list of fields you want to insert into the main document.

3. Repeat steps 1–2 for each field you want to insert into the main document.

4. Choose **File, Save** to save the main document now that it contains the source data fields and click the [🖫 Save] button.

Merge Documents

1. Click the [Merge...] button on the Mail Merge toolbar.

2. Click the [Merge] button in the Merge dialog box. Word creates a new Form Letters document that contains all the merged letters.

3. Move through the merged document to verify the merged fields from the data to the main document.

4. Click the [🖫 Save] button to save the Form Letters document, and then click the [Print] button to print the mail merge.

See Also Envelopes, Templates

MARGINS

see Page Setup   pg 245

MOVE TEXT

You can reorganize text in a Word document by moving items as you work. This method can be faster than cutting and pasting text.

Quick Tips	
Feature	*Keyboard Shortcut*
Move Text	F2

Move Text to a New Location

1. Select the text you want to move.
2. Press and hold down the left mouse button over the selected text, and drag the pointer to the new location.
3. Release the mouse button to drop the text into the new location.

See Also Copy and Cut, Objects, Paste

NEW DOCUMENT

Word presents a new blank document each time you start the application. You can create another new document at any time.

Quick Tips		
Feature	*Button*	*Keyboard Shortcut*
New Document	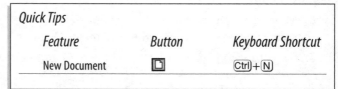	Ctrl+N

Create a New Document

1. Click the **New** ▢ button on the Standard toolbar and Word opens a new document.

Use a New Document Sample or Wizard

1. Choose **File**, **New** to open the New dialog box.
2. Select the tab that corresponds with the type of document you want to create and review the available options.
3. Double-click either the sample document to begin inserting the new text or the sample wizard and follow the steps, filling in information as necessary. Click the ▭Next >▭ button to move through the wizard answering options; then click the ▭Finish▭ button when you have completed the wizard.

See Also Open Document, Styles, Templates

NORMAL VIEW
see Views   pg 253

NUMBERED LISTS

Numbered lists are useful for presenting a series of items when they need to be kept in a sequential order.

Number Existing Text

1. Select the text you want to number.
2. Click the **Numbering** 🗒 button on the Formatting toolbar. Notice that a number is added to each paragraph, not each sentence.

Number New Text

1. Click the **Numbering** 🗒 button on the Formatting toolbar and begin typing.
2. Click the **Numbering** 🗒 button again when you no longer want numbers.

Alter Numbers

1. Select the numbered text you want to alter.
2. Choose **Format, Bullets and Numbering; Numbered** tab.
3. Double-click the type of numbers you want to display.

See Also Bulleted Lists

OBJECTS

A Word object can be any of numerous types of elements
that you add to your document: file, art, chart, worksheet,
photo, movie, text clip, and so on.

Insert a New Object

1. Choose **Insert, Object; Create New** tab.
2. Click the **Object Type** from the list box. Click the
   [OK] button to accept changes and return to the
   document.
3. Click directly on the object and make any changes to it
   using the associated toolbar.

Insert an Object File

1. Choose **Insert, Object; Create from File** tab.
2. Type in the **File Name** or click the [Browse...] button to select the file from a specific location.
3. Select the **Link to File** option if you want the object to
   be linked to this document and the source file. This
   means that any changes you make in the source file will
   be reflected in your document. Click the [OK] button to accept changes and return to the document.

TIP

An excellent use of this feature is to insert an existing Excel
spreadsheet into a Word document to create a chart. For example, a monthly report might always need to include a chart that
comes from up-to-date data that is kept in Excel.

Resize Objects

1. Click once directly on an object and the object handles
   appear on all sides and corners of the object.
2. Move the mouse pointer over one of the handles. When
   the pointer becomes a two-headed arrow, click and hold
   the handle.

3. Drag the handle to the desired size. If you drag from the corner handles, the height and width increase or decrease proportionately. If you drag from the side handles, either the height or width increases or decreases. Click elsewhere in the document to deselect the object.

Move Objects

1. Click once directly on an object and the object handles appear on all sides and corners of the object.

2. Move the mouse pointer over the object. When the pointer appears with a gray box below it, click and hold the pointer. Drag the object to the new location and drop the object.

Delete Objects

1. Click once directly on an object and the object handles appear on all sides and corners of the object.

2. Press the Del key and the object is removed from the document.

TIP

If you link a worksheet object in your document, you can quickly edit or open the source file by double-clicking the object. You can also copy, cut, and paste an object to a different location.

See Also Clip Art, Drawing Tools, Excel Worksheets

OPEN DOCUMENT

Each time you want to work with a document, you need to open it using the Open dialog box.

Quick Tips

Feature	Button	Keyboard Shortcut
Open Document	🗁	Ctrl+O or Ctrl+F12 or Ctrl+Alt+F2

Open a Document

1. Click the **Open** 🖻 button on the Standard toolbar to display the Open dialog box listing the saved Word documents.

2. Click the **Places Bar** option for the location of the file you want to open.

3. Click the **Look In** drop-down list box to help locate the correct file or drive. You can also click the **Up One Folder** 🖭 button to move through folders.

4. Double-click the file you want to open and Word opens the document.

Open Files of Different Types

1. Click the **Open** 🖻 button on the Standard toolbar to display the Open dialog box listing the saved Word documents.

2. Click the **Files of Type** drop-down list box and select the file type. The Open dialog box displays only files that are of the type you selected.

3. Double-click the file you want to open and Word opens the document. If the file cannot be opened because there is a type mismatch, Word alerts you of this with a message box.

See Also New Document, Templates

ORIENTATION
see Page Setup   pg 245

OUTLINE

Word's outline features assign preset styles to headings and normal text. You can easily create an outline with the Outlining toolbar.

Quick Tips

Feature	Button	Keyboard Shortcut
Outline Collapse	▬	Alt + ⇧Shift + - or Alt + ⇧Shift + Num Lock -
Outline Demote	➡	Alt + ⇧Shift + →
Outline Expand	➕	Alt + ⇧Shift + = or Alt + ⇧Shift + Num Lock +
Outline Move Down	⬇	Alt + ⇧Shift + ↓
Outline Move Up	⬆	Alt + ⇧Shift + ↑
Outline Promote	⬅	Alt + ⇧Shift + ←
Outline Show First Line	▤	Alt + ⇧Shift + L
Outline Show All	➡	Alt + ⇧Shift + A

Create an Outline

1. Click the **Outline View** 📄 button to switch to Outline view. Or, choose **View**, **Outline**. The Outlining toolbar appears automatically.

2. Type in your text and click the Outlining toolbar buttons to alter your text as headings or normal text. Save your document as you normally would and switch to alternate views if necessary.

See Also Fonts, Styles, Views, Workspace

PAGE BREAK
see Breaks   pg 232

P 56

PAGE NUMBERS

Word can automatically insert page numbers in your documents and print the page numbers in the position you specify.

Insert Page Numbers

1. Choose **Insert**, **Page Numbers** to open the Page Numbers dialog box.

2. Click the **Position** drop-down arrow to select whether you want the page number at the top or bottom of the page.

3. Click the **Alignment** drop-down arrow to select whether you want the page number at the left, center, or right side of the page, or on the inside or outside of the page.

4. Click the [OK] button to accept changes and return to the document. You can see the page number (grayed out) in Print Layout view.

TIP

If you don't want a page number on the first page, click to remove the check mark from the **Show Number on First Page** check box of the Page Numbers dialog box.

See Also Headers and Footers, Views

PAGE SETUP

You can adjust the page margins, orientation, paper size, and paper source for documents. All these settings can be applied to a particular section, an entire document, or from the current cursor point forward.

Set Margins

1. Choose **File, Page Setup; Margins** tab. You can also double-click the gray area of the horizontal ruler.
2. Type in or use the spin box controls to set the **Top, Bottom, Left**, and **Right** margins, and **Gutter** (left margin space for document binding).
3. Type in or use the spin box controls to set the size of the **Header** and **Footer** from the edge.
4. Click the OK button to accept changes and return to the document.

Change from Portrait to Landscape

1. Choose **File, Page Setup; Paper Size** tab.
2. Select the **Orientation** of **Portrait** or **Landscape**. Click the OK button to accept changes and return to the document.

Select the Paper Size

1. Choose **File, Page Setup; Paper Size** tab.
2. Select the **Paper Size** from the drop-down list box. The Width and Height options change automatically, although you can alter them with the spin box controls. Click the OK button to accept changes and return to the document.

Select the Paper Source

1. Choose **File, Page Setup; Paper Source** tab.
2. Select which printer tray you want the **First Page** to come from. This is convenient if you want the first page of a document to have special paper, such as letterhead.
3. Select which printer tray you want the **Other Pages** to come from. Click the OK button to accept changes and return to the document.

See Also Alignment, Breaks, Columns, Print, Print Preview

PARAGRAPH SPACING

Word enables you to set the amount of vertical space between paragraphs.

> *Quick Tips*
>
> | Feature | Keyboard Shortcut |
> | --- | --- |
> | Open or Close Up Paragraph | Ctrl + O |

Alter Paragraph Spacing

1. Select the text for which you want to alter the spacing. Or, click somewhere in the paragraph.
2. Choose **Format, Paragraphs; Indents and Spacing** tab.
3. Click the **Spacing Before** and **After** spin boxes and select the point size you want.
4. Click the OK button to accept changes and return to the workbook.

See Also Character Spacing, Line Spacing, Fonts, Text

PASTE

P
Q
R

You can share information within and between documents in Word by pasting text and objects. You can now paste up to 12 items from the Clipboard at a time. The Clipboard is where items are stored after you copy or cut them.

> *Quick Tips*
>
> | Feature | Button | Keyboard Shortcut |
> | --- | --- | --- |
> | Paste | 📋 | Ctrl + V or ◆Shift + Insert |
> | Paste Format | | Ctrl + ◆Shift + V |

Paste Text or Objects

1. Place the cursor in the location where you want to place the text or object. You must have already cut or copied text or an object for the **Paste** 🖫 button to be active.

2. Click the **Paste** 🖫 button on the Standard toolbar.

Paste Multiple Items

1. Choose **View, Toolbars, Clipboard** to open the Clipboard toolbar. You must have already cut or copied text or an object for there to be any items on the Clipboard.

2. Place the cursor in the location where you want to insert a clip item.

Paste all items in the document.

Copy an item to the Clipboard.  Delete all items from the Clipboard.

Paste an item into the document.

3. Move the mouse pointer over the Clipboard items and a ScreenTip displays what is contained in each clip (unless the clip is extensive, then only part of it displays).

4. Click the clip that you want to paste. When finished, click the **Close** ☒ button to close the Clipboard toolbar.

Paste Special

1. Place the cursor in the location where you want to place the text or object. You must have already cut or copied text or an object.

2. Choose **Edit, Paste Special** to open the Paste Special dialog box.

3. Select the **Paste** option to paste the item; select **Paste Link** to create a shortcut link to the source file (any changes you make to the source are reflected in your document). The **Paste Link** option won't be available if your copied selection isn't linkable.

4. Select the **As** option for how you want to paste the item. The **Result** area of the dialog box explains each type of paste. Click the [OK] button to accept the changes and return to the document.

See Also Copy and Cut, Hyperlink, Move Text, Replace Text

PORTRAIT
see Page Setup   pg 245

PRINT

Word makes it easy to print a document and enables you to select the printer and document settings.

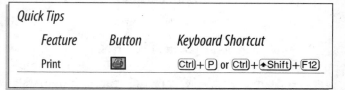

Quick Tips		
Feature	*Button*	*Keyboard Shortcut*
Print	🖨	Ctrl+P or Ctrl+Shift+F12

Print Current Document Defaults

Click the [Print] button on the Standard toolbar; the document prints according to the settings in your page setup.

Choose a Different Printer

1. Choose **File, Print** to open the Print dialog box.

2. Click the **Name** drop-down list and select the printer you want to print to.

Enter Print Options

1. Choose **File, Print** to open the Print dialog box.

Print all pages in the document.

Print the page where your cursor is currently located.

Print any page numbers and/or page range you list.

Print only the text that you selected before you opened the Print dialog box.

Specify particular items in your document to be printed.

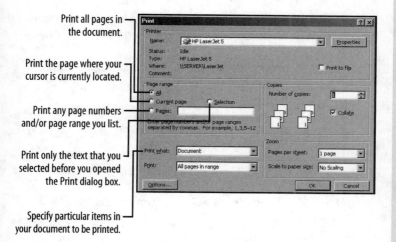

2. Select the **Page Range** that you want as your print job. Select the **Number of Copies** you want printed, and decide whether you want Word to **Collate** a multiple page document. Click the ____OK____ button to send the print job to the printer.

TIP

After you have selected to print, the printing icon in the status bar displays the number of pages as it sends them to the printer. Double-clicking this icon while it is still sending to the printer immediately cancels the print job.

See Also Page Setup, Print Preview

PRINT PREVIEW

Print Preview enables you to see document pages onscreen as they will appear printed on paper, displaying page numbers, headers, footers, fonts, font sizes and styles, orientation, and margins.

Quick Tips		
Feature	*Button*	*Keyboard Shortcut*
Print Preview	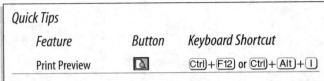	Ctrl+F12 or Ctrl+Alt+I

Preview a Document

1. Click the **Print Preview** button on the Standard toolbar.

2. Click the **Multiple Pages** button on the Print Preview toolbar and click the number of pages you want to view at a time. Click the **One Page** button on the Print Preview toolbar to return to viewing one page.

3. Click directly on the previewed document and the magnification increases. Click directly on the previewed document again and the magnification returns to the original percentage.

4. Click the Close button on the Print Preview toolbar to return to the document.

Edit in Print Preview

1. Click the **Magnifier** button on the Print Preview toolbar.

2. Click anywhere in the previewed document and type your edits.

3. Click the **Magnifier** button again when finished making your edits.

See Also Page Setup, Print, Views, Workspace

P
Q
R

PRINT LAYOUT VIEW
see Views pg 253

REDO
see Undo pg 252

REPLACE TEXT

In Word, you can replace text, character, and paragraph formatting, and special characters.

Quick Tips	
Feature	*Keyboard Shortcut*
Replace	Ctrl + H

Search and Replace Text

1. Choose **Edit**, **Replace** to open the Find and Replace dialog box.
2. Type the text you want to locate in the **Find What** text box. Any text from a previous search will still be in the dialog box, unless you have exited Word.
3. Click in the **Replace With** text box (or press the Tab↹ key) and type the text you want to replace it with.
4. Select from the Search and Replace options.

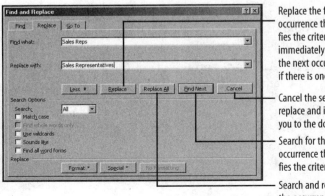

Replace the first occurrence that satisfies the criterion and immediately move to the next occurrence, if there is one.

Cancel the search and replace and it returns you to the document.

Search for the next occurrence that satisfies the criterion.

Search and replace all the occurrences that satisfy the criterion.

5. Click the [OK] button when Word tells you how many replacements were made. If there is no text that satisfies the criteria, Word alerts you with a message box.

Perform an Advanced Replace

1. Choose **Edit, Replace** to open the Find and Replace dialog box.

2. Click the [More ∓] button to expand the **Search Options** in the dialog box.

3. Type the text you want to locate in the **Find What** and **Replace With** text boxes. Any text from a previous search will still be in the dialog box unless you have exited Word.

4. Select from the various **Search Options** for the find and replace items:

   - **Match Case**—For example, instead of finding all occurrences of lowercased **sales**, you can search specifically for initial-capped **Sales**.

   - **Find Whole Words Only**—For example, **this** will find **the** instead of also finding **them** and **they** (this is inactive if there are multiple words).

   - **Use Wildcards**—For example, this will find character occurrences using the following *wildcards*: **? * [ ]**. R?t will find **rot** and **rat**; r*t will find **replenishment** and **rut**; r[ao]t will find **rot**, **rat**, and **root**.

   - **Sounds Like**—For example, this will find phonetically similar text, such as **too**, **to**, **two**.

   - **Find All Word Forms**—For example, this will find different word forms, such as **eat**, **ate**, **eaten**.

5. Click the [Format ▾] button to select a particular format; click the [Special ▾] button to select particular characters for the find and replace items.

6. Select from the Find and Replace buttons. Click the
   OK button when Word tells you how many
   replacements were made. If there is no text that satisfies
   the criteria, Word alerts you with a message box.

7. Click the Cancel button to exit the Find and Replace
   dialog box.

See Also Copy and Cut, Find, Paste, Redo

RULERS
see Columns   pg 233

SAVE DOCUMENTS

Save the document you are working in to store it for later
retrieval. A good practice is to save your documents frequently as you work in them.

Quick Tips			
Feature	*Button*	*Keyboard Shortcut*	
Save		Ctrl + S or ◆Shift + F12	
		or Alt + ◆Shift + F2	
Save As		F12	

Save a Document

1. Click the **Save** button on the Standard toolbar to
   save any recent changes. If you haven't saved the document yet, the Save As dialog box appears.

2. Click the **Places Bar** option for the location of the file you want to save. Click the **Save In** drop-down list box to help locate the correct folder or drive. You can also click the **Up One Folder** 🖻 button to move through folders.

3. Type the **File Name** and click the 🔒 Save button.

Save As a Different Name

1. Choose **File, Save As** to open the Save As dialog box.

2. Click the **Places Bar** option for the location of the file you want to save. Click the **Save In** drop-down list box to help locate the correct folder or drive. You can also click the **Up One Folder** 🖻 button to move through folders.

3. Type the new **File Name** and click the 🔒 Save button.

Save As a Different File Type

1. Choose **File, Save As** to open the Save As dialog box.

2. Click the **Places Bar** option for the location of the file you want to save. Click the **Save In** drop-down list box to help locate the correct folder or drive. You can also click the **Up One Folder** 🖻 button to move through folders.

3. Click the **Save As Type** drop-down list box and select the desired file type. Type the **File Name** and click the 🔲 Save button.

See Also Close Documents, Open Documents, Versions, Web Pages

SEARCH
see Find   pg 239

SECTIONS
see Breaks   pg 232

SHADING

You can apply colors and shades to the background of selected text. You can also follow the same steps to change the text shade to something different.

Shade Text

1. Select the text that you want to shade.
2. Choose **Format, Borders and Shading; Shading** tab.
3. Select a color in the **Fill** area and click the **Style** drop-down list box to apply a pattern to the background of the text. You can also click the **Color** drop-down list to select the pattern. Click the OK button to accept changes and return to the document.

See Also Borders, Fonts

SHARE AND PROTECT DOCUMENTS

You can share documents either by restricting access to the document or preventing changes from being made within each particular document.

Set File Share Options

1. Choose **Tools, Options; Save** tab.
2. Select the **File Sharing Options** for your document.

Any user will need to enter this password to open this document.

Any other user can open the document but changes made must be saved with a different filename.

Any user can open the document but will need to enter this password to make any edits.

3. Type and reenter any passwords that need to be confirmed when Word provides a Confirm Password dialog box and click the `OK` button. Click the `OK` button in the Options dialog box to accept changes and return to the document.

Protect a Document

1. Choose **Tools, Protect Document** to open the Protect Document dialog box.

2. Select the options of what to Protect Document For.

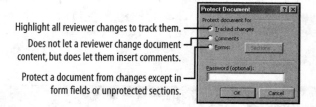

Highlight all reviewer changes to track them.

Does not let a reviewer change document content, but does let them insert comments.

Protect a document from changes except in form fields or unprotected sections.

3. Type and reenter any passwords that need to be confirmed when Word provides a Confirm Password dialog box, and click the `OK` button. Click the `OK` button in the Protect Document dialog box to accept changes and return to the document.

See Also Comments, Track Changes

SPACING

see Character Spacing   pg 232

SPELLING AND GRAMMAR

Word 2000 shows red wavy lines under any misspelled
words and green wavy lines under any sentences that are
grammatically problematic.

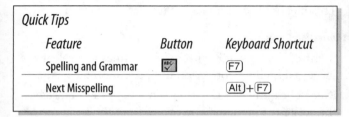

Quick Tips

Feature	Button	Keyboard Shortcut
Spelling and Grammar	ABC✓	F7
Next Misspelling		Alt + F7

Check Spelling and Grammar

1. Click the **Spelling and Grammar** ABC✓ button on the
   Standard toolbar. The Spelling and Grammar dialog
   box opens, displaying the first spelling or grammar error
   it finds.

2. Click the appropriate spelling option in the **Suggestions**
   list box; if one doesn't work, type the change directly in
   the **Not in Dictionary** list box.

3. Click the appropriate button to make the selected
   Suggestions change.

A word that shouldn't be altered and it should
not flag any other instances of the word.

A word that shouldn't
be altered.

Add a word to the dictionary
so it will remember the word
as correct in the future.

Make the selected
Suggestions change.

Make the selected **Suggestions**
change throughout the document.

Add the spelling error and
the correction to the
AutoCorrect list to correct
automatically as you type.

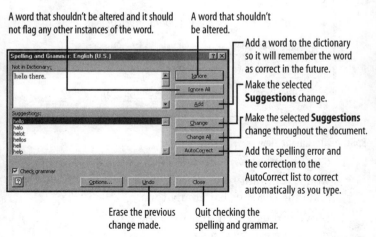

Erase the previous
change made.

Quit checking the
spelling and grammar.

4. Click the [Yes] or [No] button if Word asks you to continue checking the document; especially if you didn't start checking at the beginning of the document.

5. Click the [OK] button if Word displays a message telling you the spelling and grammar check is complete. This means all inaccuracies have been reviewed.

In-Text Correction

1. Right-click any words with red wavy lines and select the suggested spelling correction from the shortcut menu.

2. Right-click any words with green wavy lines and select the suggested grammar correction from the shortcut menu.

See Also Thesaurus

SPLIT WINDOW

You can simultaneously view two parts of document if you split the window into two panes. This is convenient when you need to view information at the beginning of a document in order to work in another portion of the document.

Quick Tips	
Feature	*Keyboard Shortcut*
Close Split Pane	Alt + ⬆Shift + C
Split Document	Alt + Ctrl + S
Other Pane	F6 or ⬆Shift + F6

Split the Document View

1. Choose **Window, Split** and click in the document where you want to view the split area. You can click and drag the split bar at any time.

2. Move through each split with the scrollbars to position the document view areas.

3. Double-click the split bar to return to viewing one part of the document; or choose **Window, Remove Split**.

See Also View Multiple Documents, Views, Workspace

STYLES

Word 2000 has numerous default styles for you to choose from when formatting text. Instead of applying a particular format to text, you can apply a style that formats the text the same way each time.

Quick Tips	
Feature	*Keyboard Shortcut*
Style	Ctrl + ⬆Shift + S
Normal Style	Ctrl + ⬆Shift + N
Reset Characters	Ctrl + Spacebar or
	Ctrl + ⬆Shift + Z
Reset Paragraph	Ctrl + Q
Apply Heading 1	Ctrl + Alt + 1
Apply Heading 2	Ctrl + Alt + 2
Apply Heading 3	Ctrl + Alt + 3

Apply a Word Style

1. Select the text you want to style.
2. Click the **Style** drop-down list to select the style you want to apply.

Create a New Style

1. Select the text you want to format as a style. Then, format the text the way you want it to appear in the style.
2. Type the new name in the **Style** drop-down list box area and press the ⏎Enter key. Click the **Style** drop-down arrow to see your new style listed.

TIP

The next time you exit Word, you will be notified that you made a change to your global Word template and asked whether you want to save the changes.

See Also Fonts, New Document, Templates, Text

SYMBOLS

The Symbol command enables you to insert symbols, special characters, and international characters.

Quick Tips

Feature	Keyboard Shortcut
Symbol Font	Ctrl + ⇧Shift + Q
Em Dash	Alt + Ctrl + ⌧ Num Lock −
En Dash	Ctrl + ⌧ Num Lock −
Nonbreaking Hyphen	Ctrl + ⎯
Optional Hyphen	Ctrl + −
Nonbreaking Space	Ctrl + ⇧Shift + Spacebar
Copyright	Alt + Ctrl + C
Registered	Alt + Ctrl + R
Trademark	Alt + Ctrl + T
Ellipsis	Alt + Ctrl + .
Single Opening Quote	Ctrl + ', '
Single Closing Quote	Ctrl + ', '
Double Opening Quote	Ctrl + ', "
Double Closing Quote	Ctrl + ', "

Insert a Symbol

1. Click the cursor in the text where you want to add the symbol.

2. Choose **Insert, Symbol; Symbols** tab. You can locate different symbols and different types of symbols by

clicking the **Font** drop-down arrow and selecting from the different fonts. Each font provides you with a different symbol selection. Choose **(Normal Text)** and the appropriate **Subset** language to enter foreign characters.

3. Click the **Special Characters** tab to select from different types of special characters.

4. Double-click the symbol you want to insert into your document. Click the **Close** ☒ button to return to the document.

TIP

To delete a symbol, select the symbol and press the Del key.

See Also Fonts, Search Text, Replace Text

TABLES

Instead of creating long lists of information and trying to cross-reference these lists, you can add a table to your document.

Quick Tips

Feature	Keyboard Shortcut
End of Column	Alt + PgDn
End of Row	Alt + End
Column Break	Ctrl + Shift + Enter
Next Cell	Tab
Previous Cell	Shift + Tab
Start of Column	Alt + PgUp
Start of Row	Alt + Home

Draw Table

1. Click the **Tables and Borders Toolbars** 🔲 button on the Standard toolbar; the pointer becomes a pencil and the Tables and Borders toolbar opens.

2. Click in the document and drag to draw the outer border of the table. Click inside the table and draw the rows and columns.

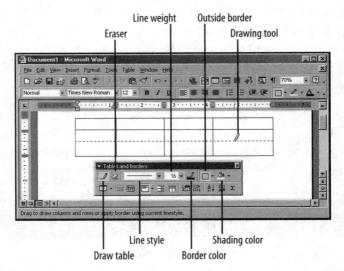

Line weight   Outside border

Eraser   Drawing tool

Line style   Shading color

Draw table   Border color

3. Click the **Draw Table** button on the Tables and Borders toolbar, which converts the pointer to a cursor so that you can add data to the table. Click the **Close** button to close the Tables and Borders toolbar, or choose **View, Toolbars, Tables and Borders** to toggle the toolbar closed.

Insert Table

1. Click the **Insert Table** button on the Standard toolbar and select the number of rows and columns you want from the drop-down box.

2. Click the cursor in the table cells and type to add the data.

Alter Table Text Wrapping

1. Click in the table you want to position in your document.

2. Choose **Table, Table Properties; Table** tab.

3. Select the **Text Wrapping** option (**Around** will wrap document text around the table). Click the [OK] button to accept changes and return to the document.

Work with Columns

1. Move the mouse pointer over the right edge of the column you want to alter. When the mouse pointer changes into a two-headed arrow, click and drag the column to the new size.

2. Click the top border of a column (when the pointer becomes a black down arrow) to select it. Right-click and choose **Insert Columns** from the shortcut menu to add a column to the left of the selected column.

3. Right-click the column again and choose **Distribute Columns Evenly** from the shortcut menu to make each column the same size.

4. Right-click the column again and choose **Delete Columns** from the shortcut menu; that column is deleted.

Work with Rows

1. Move the mouse pointer over the bottom edge of the row you want to alter. When the mouse pointer changes into a two-headed arrow, click and drag the row to the new size.

2. Click the left border of a row (when the pointer becomes a white right arrow) to select it. Right-click and chose **Insert Rows** from the shortcut menu to add a row above the selected row.

3. Right-click the row again and choose **Distribute Rows Evenly** from the shortcut menu to make each row the same size.

4. Right-click the row again and choose **Delete Rows** from the shortcut menu; that row is deleted.

AutoFormat Table

1. Click in any cell of the table you want to format.

2. Choose **Table, Table AutoFormat** to open the Table AutoFormat dialog box.

3. Click an option in the **Formats** list to view a format sample in the **Preview** area. Click the ⬚ OK ⬚ button to accept changes and return to the document.

Format Text Direction

1. Select the cells for which you want to alter the text direction.

2. Choose **Format**, **Text Direction** to open the Text Direction - Table Cell dialog box.

3. Click the desired **Orientation**. Click the [OK] button to accept changes and return to the document.

TIP

To alter cell text alignment, right-click a cell and choose **Cell Alignment** from the shortcut menu. Then, click the alignment style from the submenu.

Convert Table to Text

1. Select the table you want to convert.

2. Choose **Table**, **Convert**, **Table to Text** to open the Convert Table to Text dialog box.

3. Select the **Separate Text With** option and click the [OK] button; the table is now Normal-styled text.

Convert Text to a Table

1. Select the text you want to convert.

2. Choose **Table**, **Convert**, **Text to Table** to open the Convert Text to Table dialog box.

3. Select the **Table Size** for **Number of Columns**, the **Separate Text At** option, and click the [OK] button; the text is now a table.

Sort Table Data

1. Select the table you want to sort.

2. Choose **Table**, **Sort** to open the Sort dialog box.

3. Click the **Sort By** drop-down list box to determine the initial sort.

See Also Columns

TABS

You can align tab stops in different positions and select leader types. Setting tabs is useful for indenting text at one or more tab stops.

Set a Tab Stop

1. Click in the paragraph where you want to set a tab.
2. Click the horizontal ruler tab and indent settings button to choose the type of tab.

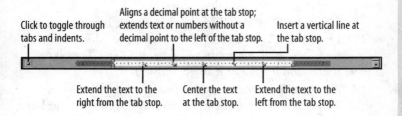

Click to toggle through tabs and indents.

Aligns a decimal point at the tab stop; extends text or numbers without a decimal point to the left of the tab stop.

Insert a vertical line at the tab stop.

Extend the text to the right from the tab stop.

Center the text at the tab stop.

Extend the text to the left from the tab stop.

3. Move the mouse pointer to the place on the ruler where you want the tab stop, and click once. Press the Tab⇄ key to align the text with the tab stop.

Delete Tab Stops

1. Click in the paragraph in which you want to delete a tab stop.
2. Click the tab stop on the ruler and drag it off the ruler.

> **TIP**
> You can move a tab stop by clicking the tab indicator on the ruler and dragging it to the desired location on the ruler.

See Also Alignment, Character Spacing, Indents, Page Setup

TEMPLATES

You can create a document template with any type of text, formatting, toolbars, macros, styles, and just about any setting you can change.

Create and Open a New Document Template

1. Click the **New** 🗋 button on the Standard toolbar to open a new document. Type in the text and format it how you want the document template to appear.

2. Click the **Save** 🖫 button on the Standard toolbar to open the Save As dialog box.

3. Click the **Save As Type** drop-down list box and select **Document Template**. Any newly created document templates will automatically default to the **Templates** folder and have a **.dot** file extension.

4. Type a **File Name** and click the 🖫 **Save** button. You can make modifications to this document template at any time, just make sure you save the changes. Click the **Close** ✕ button to close the document.

5. Choose **File, New; General** tab. Click the document template you just created.

6. Click the **Create New Document** option and click the ⃝ OK button to open the template as a document.

Attach a Document Template

1. Choose **Tools, Templates and Add-ins** to open the Tools and Add-ins dialog box.

2. Click the **Attach...** button and double-click the document template **File Name** from the Attach Template dialog box. This is the default document template location. If the template you want to attach is not in this folder, either move the file before continuing or locate the file and continue.

3. Click the **Automatically Update Document Styles** option so that any styles in the document template will update the styles in your current document. Click the OK button.

See Also New Document, Save Documents, Styles

TEXT

To draw attention to important text in a document, you can make the text any combination of bold, italic, and underline.

Quick Tips		
Feature	*Button*	*Keyboard Shortcut*
Bold	**B**	Ctrl+B
Italic	*I*	Ctrl+I
Underline	U	Ctrl+U
Double Underline		Ctrl+⬆Shift+D
Word Underline		Ctrl+⬆Shift+W

Bold Text

1. Select the text you want to format bold.
2. Click the **Bold** **B** button on the Formatting toolbar; click the **Bold** **B** button again to remove the bold.

Italicize Text

1. Select the text you want to format italic.
2. Click the **Italic** *I* button on the Formatting toolbar; click the **Italic** *I* button again to remove the italic.

Underline Text

1. Select the text you want to format underlined.
2. Click the **Underline** U button on the Formatting toolbar, and then click the **Underline** U button again to remove the underline.

Highlight Text

1. Select the text that you want to highlight.
2. Click the **Highlight** drop-down list box on the Formatting toolbar and select the desired color; click **None** to have no highlight. Keep in mind that high-lighted text prints as gray on a black-and-white printer.

See Also Alignment, Character Spacing, Fonts

THEMES
see Web Pages   pg 253

THESAURUS

Word's Thesaurus is a convenient tool that helps you replace words with more suitable ones.

Quick Tips

Feature	Keyboard Shortcut
Thesaurus	(⬆Shift)+(F7)

Use the Thesaurus

1. Choose **Tools, Language, Thesaurus** to look up the word nearest the cursor in the Thesaurus dialog box.
2. Click the synonym you want for the word in the **Replace with Synonym** list box. Click the [Look Up] button to look up another word in the **Meanings** list.
3. Click the [Replace] button to insert the new word; the Thesaurus dialog box then disappears.

See Also Spelling and Grammar

TRACK CHANGES

Sometimes you find that you have to make corrections in a document, or perhaps you are working on a report in a team environment. To determine who made what changes when, you can track the changes onscreen with revision marks.

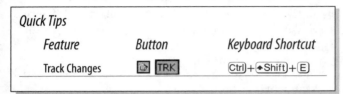

Quick Tips

Feature	Button	Keyboard Shortcut
Track Changes	TRK	Ctrl+Shift+E

Track Document Changes

1. Right-click the **Track Changes** TRK indicator on the status bar and choose **Track Changes** from the shortcut menu.

2. Type some changes into the document. The new text appears as a different color and underlined. Any changes to a line are flagged by a vertical black bar in the margin.

Alter Viewable Changes

1. Choose **Tools, Track Changes, Highlight Changes** to open the Highlight Changes dialog box.

2. Select from the available tracking options.

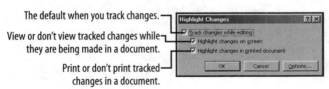

The default when you track changes.

View or don't view tracked changes while they are being made in a document.

Print or don't print tracked changes in a document.

3. Click the Options... button to alter the track changes colors according to inserted text, deleted text, changed formatting, or changed lines. This is convenient when multiple people are editing a document; they can each be assigned a different color.

4. Click the OK button in both dialog boxes to accept changes and return to the document.

Compare Two Documents

1. Open the document in which you want the comparison made; this will be the *new document*.

2. Choose **Tools, Track Changes, Compare Documents**.

3. Locate the **File Name** of the *original* file you want to compare with the new document and click the `Open` button. Any old text appears in a different color with strikethrough; any new text appears in a different color.

See Also Accept and Reject Changes, Comments, Share and Protect Documents, Versions

TYPEFACE
see Fonts   pg 239

UNDERLINE
see Text   pg 250

UNDO AND REDO

Undo and Redo are convenient when you want to see how your document looks with and without changes you make.

Quick Tips		
Feature	*Button*	*Keyboard Shortcut*
Undo	↶	Ctrl+Z or Alt+←Backspace
Redo or Repeat	↷	Ctrl+Y or Alt+↑Shift+←Backspace or F4 or Alt+↵Enter

Use Undo and Redo

1. Type or make change(s) in your document.

2. Click the **Undo** ↶ button as many times as necessary to undo the change(s).

3. Click the **Redo** ⟳ button as many times as necessary to redo the change(s).

TIP

You can also click the **Undo** or **Redo** drop-down list arrows to select the exact changes you want to make. In addition, this can be convenient when you have made an error in your worksheet.

See Also Close Documents, Save Documents

VERSIONS

Because you are archiving document versions, you cannot go back and modify a saved version of a document. Before you can modify an earlier version, you must open that version and use the **Save As** command to save it as a separate file.

Save Document Versions

1. Choose **File, Versions** to open the Versions dialog box.

2. Click the **Automatically Save a Version on Close** option if you want a different version to save each time you close the document.

3. Click the ⟦ Save Now... ⟧ button to open the Save Version dialog box, type any notes in the **Comments on Version** text box, and click the ⟦ OK ⟧ button. If you haven't saved the document yet, you are prompted with a Save As dialog box. Type a **File Name** and click the ⟦ 💾 Save ⟧ button. If you have saved the document already, click the ⟦ Close ⟧ button to return to the document.

Review Existing Versions

1. Open the document that you have saved a document version of. Choose **File, Versions** to open the Versions dialog box.

2. Click one of the **Existing Versions** and click the [Open] button to view the document; click the [View Comments...] button to review your version notes; click the [Delete] button to delete the version. Click the [Close] button to return to the document.

TIP

You cannot modify a saved version of a document unless you open a particular version and save it with a different filename.

See Also Comments, Save Documents, Share and Protect Documents, Track Changes

VIEW MULTIPLE DOCUMENTS

If you don't want to constantly switch between documents, you can view multiple Word documents onscreen. The document displaying a darker title bar is considered the active document; when you type, text appears there.

View Multiple Documents

1. Open all the documents you want to simultaneously view.

2. Choose **Window, Arrange All**. All open documents are automatically arranged next to each other.

3. Click the title bar or click in the body of the document you want to work in.

TIP

To return to viewing only one entire document, double-click the title bar of the document you want to work in.

See Also Open Documents, Split Windows, Workspace

VIEWS

Word provides many ways to view documents—each view has its purpose.

Quick Tips

Feature	Button	Keyboard Shortcut
Normal View	▤	Ctrl+Alt+N
Web Layout View	▣	Ctrl+Alt+W
Print Layout View	▣	Ctrl+Alt+P
Outline View	▤	Ctrl+Alt+O

Switch Document Views

Choose the view button to the left of the horizontal scrollbar according to the view you desire.

Best view for how a Web document will appear.

Default view for typing, editing, and formatting text. Best for organizing and developing the structure of your document in an outline format.

Display the document as it will print.

See Also Document Map, Print Preview, View Multiple Documents, Web Pages, Workspace

WEB LAYOUT VIEW
see Views   pg 253

WEB PAGES

You can view your documents as Web pages in Web Page Preview even before you have saved the file as a Web page.

> **Quick Tips**
>
> | Feature | Button | Keyboard Shortcut |
> |---|---|---|
> | Web Go Back | ⇦ | Alt + ⇦ |
> | Web Go Forward | ⇨ | Alt + ⇨ |

Use Web Page Preview

Choose, **File**, **Web Page Preview** to open the Internet Explorer browser and display the document. Click the **Back** ⇦ button to return to the Word document.

Save As a Web Page

1. Choose **File**, **Save As Web Page** to open the Save As dialog box.

2. Click the **Places Bar** option for the location of the file you want to save. Click the **Save In** drop-down list box to help locate the correct folder or drive. You can also click the **Up One Folder** 🖻 button to move through folders.

3. Click the Change Title... button and type in a **Page Title** if you want the Web page title to be different than the filename, and click the OK button. Type the **File Name** and click the 🖫 Save button.

Apply a Document Background Color or Fill Effect

1. Choose **Format**, **Background**, and select the color you want to apply or select the **Fill Effects** command to open the Fill Effects dialog box.

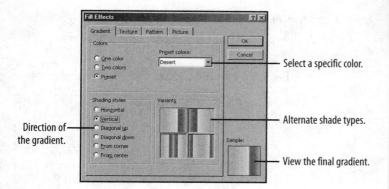

Direction of the gradient.

Select a specific color.

Alternate shade types.

View the final gradient.

2. Choose between the **Gradient**, **Texture**, **Pattern**, and **Picture** tabs to apply different effects in the Fill Effects dialog box. The **Sample** window in the bottom right of the dialog box shows you what your background will look like. Click the `OK` button to accept changes and return to the document.

Insert Frames

1. Choose **Format**, **Frames**, **Table of Contents in Frame** to insert a document frame with a table of contents.

2. Click the `Save` button if you are asked to save any changes in your document. Any Word-styled headers become hyperlinks in the table of contents to the section in the document.

3. Click in the frame where you want to add another frame. Choose **View**, **Toolbars**, **Frames** to open the Frames toolbar if it isn't already open.

Delete a frame.

Open the frame properties.

4. Click the appropriate frame button on the Frames toolbar. Type the information you want in the new frame. Click the **Close** ☒ button to close the Frames toolbar, or choose **View**, **Toolbars**, **Frames** to toggle the toolbar closed.

Apply a Document Theme

1. Click in the document (or particular frame) where you want to apply a theme.

2. Choose **Format, Theme** to open the Theme dialog box.

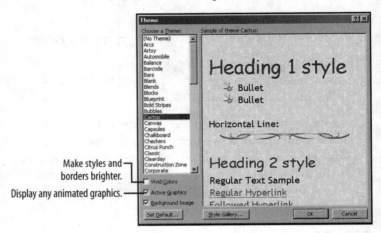

Make styles and borders brighter.

Display any animated graphics.

3. Click a theme in the **Choose a Theme** list box. Click the OK button and apply the theme to your document.

See Also Views

WILDCARD

see Replace Text   pg 247

WORD COUNT

Word provides statistics about your documents so that you can track the number of pages, words, characters, paragraphs, and lines.

Find Word Count

1. Choose **Tools, Word Count** to open the Word Count dialog box.

2. Click the Cancel button when you finish reviewing the **Statistics**.

See Also Spelling and Grammar

WORKSPACE

You can click the scrollbars to move the view of the document; press the keys on the keyboard to move the cursor through the document; or view the rulers or full screen.

Quick Tips		
Feature	**Button**	**Keyboard Shortcut**
Minimize Document Window	▭	
Maximize Document window	▢	Ctrl + F10
Move Document Window		Ctrl + F7
Restore Document Window	◲	Ctrl + F5
Size Document Window		Ctrl + F8

Use Scrollbar Options

1. Click the **Up** and **Down** scrollbar arrows to scroll through the document. Click directly on the large scrollbar and drag it up and down to quickly move through the document.

2. Click the **Previous Find/Go To** ⬆ and **Next Find/Go To** ⬇ buttons to move through the document by page.

3. Click the **Select Browse Object** ⬤ to browse through the document using different features: **Go To**; **Find**; **Browse by Edits**, **Heading**, **Graphic**, **Table**, **Field**, **Endnote**, **Footnote**, **Comment**, **Section**, or **Page**.

Increase Document View Size

1. Click the **Zoom** drop-down list on the Standard toolbar.

2. Select the percentage or descriptive size you want to view your document in. You can also click directly on the **Zoom** list box and type in an exact zoom percentage.

View Rulers

Choose **View, Rulers** to toggle between the rulers being displayed or not.

View Full Screen

1. Choose **View, Full Screen** to view the document with only the Full Screen toolbar to close the full screen. You can move the mouse pointer to the top of the screen and the menu commands appear.

2. Press the Esc key or click the Close Full Screen button to return to the previous view.

See Also Document Map, Views

PART 3

EXCEL QUICK REFERENCE

ACCEPT OR REJECT CHANGES

When you are ready to finalize tracked changes in a workbook, you determine which changes to accept and which to
reject.

Quick Tips		
Feature	*Button*	*Keyboard Shortcut*
Revision Marks Toggle	TRK	Ctrl + ↑Shift + E

Review Tracked Changes

1. Choose **Tools, Track Changes, Accept or Reject
   Changes**. Click the ⟨ OK ⟩ button in the message box
   that appears telling you this action will save the workbook, unless you just recently saved the workbook.

2. Click the ⟨ OK ⟩ button to accept the default options
   in the list boxes for **When, Who,** and **Where** you want
   to accept or reject a change.

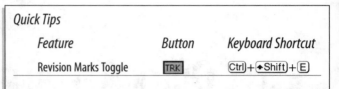

Accept the selected change. — Accept — Reject — Accept All — Reject All — Close — Stop reviewing tracked changes.

Reject the selected change. — Accept all changes in the worksheet. — Reject all changes in the worksheet.

3. Click the appropriate button to accept or reject each or
   all changes. Notice that the comment marker remains
   in the cell for your reference.

See Also Track Changes

ALIGNMENT

When you enter data into a worksheet, numbers align to the left and text aligns to the right. However, you can change the alignment of data at any time, before or after you have entered the data.

Quick Tips

Feature	Button	Keyboard Shortcut
Merge & Center		
Align Left		Ctrl+L
Align Right		Ctrl+R
Center		Ctrl+E
Increase Indent		
Decrease Indent		

Apply Text Alignment Control

1. Select the cell(s) you want to format.
2. Choose **Format, Cells; Alignment** tab.

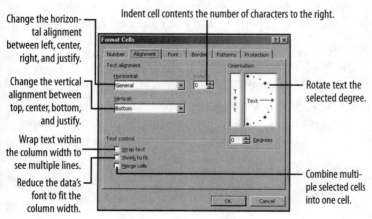

Change the horizontal alignment between left, center, right, and justify.

Indent cell contents the number of characters to the right.

Change the vertical alignment between top, center, bottom, and justify.

Rotate text the selected degree.

Wrap text within the column width to see multiple lines.

Reduce the data's font to fit the column width.

Combine multiple selected cells into one cell.

3. Click the **OK** button to accept the changes and return to the worksheet.

See Also Fonts, Text

AUTOCALCULATE

Use AutoCalculate to see a function performed on data without adding the function directly into the worksheet.

Use AutoCalculate

1. Select the cells that you want to AutoCalculate.

2. Right-click the status bar and choose the type of calculation from the shortcut menu. Excel automatically calculates the cells and displays the answer in the status bar.

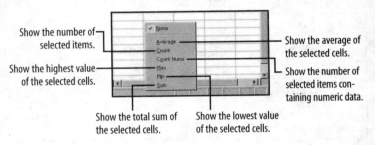

Show the number of selected items.

Show the highest value of the selected cells.

Show the average of the selected cells.

Show the number of selected items containing numeric data.

Show the total sum of the selected cells.

Show the lowest value of the selected cells.

See Also AutoSum, Formulas, Functions

AUTOFILL

AutoFill can automatically extend series types, such as dates, quarters, periods, and even number trends.

Use AutoFill

1. Type the first cell series name (or enough cells to start a number trend).

2. Click the pointer on the bottom-right cell corner when it becomes a plus sign. Drag the pointer to the number of cells in the series.

See Also Move Data, Copy and Cut, Paste

AUTOFORMAT

Excel provides the AutoFormat feature, which can format
selected cells using predefined formats.

AutoFormat

1. Select the cells you want to AutoFormat.
2. Choose **Format**, **AutoFormat** to open the AutoFormat
   dialog box. Click the AutoFormat you want in the sample
   preview area. Click the [____OK____] button to apply the
   AutoFormat to your data.

See Also Conditional Formatting, Fonts, Text

AUTOSUM

Excel can use formulas to perform calculations for you. Because
a formula refers to the cells rather than to the values, Excel
updates the sum whenever you change the values in the cells.

Use AutoSum

1. Click in the cell where you want the total of a range of
   cells to be added.
2. Click the **AutoSum** Σ button on the Standard toolbar. Excel automatically selects the most obvious range
   of numbers to calculate. You can also select the range of
   cells in advance and the calculation is placed the next
   cell over or below the selection. If that cell isn't available, it places the calculation at the closest end of the
   selected row or column of cells.
3. Press the (↵Enter) key to accept the range. The formula
   for the calculated cells is displayed in the formula bar.

See Also AutoCalculate, Formulas, Functions

AVERAGE
see Functions   pg 240

AXIS
see Charts   pg 232

BOLD
see Format   pg 239

BORDERS

You can add a border to any or all sides of a cell, selected cells, or objects. In addition, you can format the types of borders for your data.

Quick Tips	
Feature	Keyboard Shortcut
Outline Border	Ctrl + Shift + &
Remove All Borders	Ctrl + Shift + ⎵

Add Text Borders

1. Select the cells to which you want to add a border.
2. Click the **Borders** ▦ button on the Formatting toolbar and select the type of border you want to apply from the drop-down list.

Format Borders

1. Select the cells that have a border you want to format.
2. Choose **Format, Cells**; **Border** tab.
3. Select the optional **Presets, Line, Color**, and **Border**. Click the ⌷ ok ⌷ button to accept the changes and return to the worksheet.

See Also Cells, Print, Shading

CELLS

A worksheet is a grid of columns and rows. The intersection of any column and row is called a cell. Each cell in a worksheet has a unique cell reference, the designation formed by combining the row and column headings.

Quick Tips	
Feature	*Keyboard Shortcut*
Insert Blank Cells	Ctrl + ⬆Shift + +
Delete Selection	Ctrl + −

Insert Cells

1. Select the cell(s) where you want to insert new cell(s) above or to the left.

2. Choose **Insert, Cells** to open the Insert dialog box.

3. Select the **Insert** option and click the ⬚ OK ⬚ button to accept the changes and return to the worksheet.

Delete Cells

1. Select the cell(s) you want to delete.

2. Choose **Edit, Delete** to open the Delete dialog box.

3. Select the **Delete** option and click the ⬚ OK ⬚ button to accept the changes and return to the worksheet.

Clear Cells Without Delete

1. Select the cell(s) you want to clear.

2. Choose **Edit, Clear**, and choose whether you want to clear the cell **Comments**, **Contents**, **Formats**, or **All** from the submenu.

See Also Alignment, Columns, Fonts, Numbers, Rows

CHARTS

Numeric data can sometimes be difficult to interpret. Using data to create charts helps visualize the data's significance. You can quickly change the appearance of charts in Excel by clicking directly on the chart. You can change titles, legend information, axis points, category names, and more.

Quick Tips	
Feature	*Keyboard Shortcut*
Create Chart	F11
Insert Chart Sheet	Alt + F1

Create a Chart

1. Select the cells you want included in the chart.

2. Click the **Chart Wizard** button on the Standard toolbar.

3. Click the **Chart Type** and **Chart Sub-Type** in the Chart Wizard dialog box, then choose Next >.

4. Click **Rows** (or **Columns**) to choose on which data the chart will be based, then choose Next >. You can also change the data range if you selected too many, not enough, or the wrong cells.

5. Type the various titles for the chart, then choose Next >.

6. Click the option for where you want to place the chart, then choose Finish.

Change the Chart Type

1. Right-click the plot area and choose **Chart Type** from the shortcut menu.

2. Select the alternate **Chart Type** and **Chart Sub-Type** in the Chart Type dialog box.

3. Click the OK button. The updated chart type appears in the chart.

Alter Source Data Range

1. Right-click the plot area and choose **Source Data** from the shortcut menu.

2. Click directly in your worksheet and select the data range you want. The **Data Range** area automatically updates with the cells you selected.

3. Click the [OK] button. The updated data range appears in your chart.

Alter Chart Options

1. Right-click the plot area and choose **Chart Options** from the shortcut menu to open the Chart Options dialog box. Any changes you make to this dialog box automatically appear in the chart preview window on the dialog box.

2. Type in a new **Chart Title** in the **Titles** tab.

3. Click the **Axes** tab and see how altering the **Primary Axis** affects your chart.

4. Click the **Gridlines** tab and select to add **Category (X) Axis Major Gridlines**.

5. Click the **Legend** tab and see how altering the **Placement** affects your chart.

6. Click the **Data Labels** tab and see how altering the **Data Labels** affects your chart.

7. Click the **Data Table** tab and select to **Show Data Table**.

8. Click the [OK] button to accept all your chart options and see how your chart has changed.

TIP

To change the pattern and scale of the gridlines, double-click the gridline itself. Then use the Format Gridlines dialog box to make your selections and click the [OK] button.

Format the Plot Area

1. Right-click the Plot Area and choose **Format Plot Area** from the shortcut menu.

2. Select the **Area** color on the **Patterns** tab of the Format Plot Area dialog box.

3. Click the [OK] button to accept your changes and return to the chart.

Format the Chart Area

1. Right-click the **Chart Area** and choose **Format Chart Area** from the shortcut menu. Click the **Font** tab of the Format Plot Area dialog box. Select the **Font** options you want.

2. Click the **Patterns** tab and select a type of **Border** around the chart and any color you want for the chart **Area** itself. Click the [OK] button to accept your changes and return to the chart.

Format the Axis Scale

1. Right-click the Value Axis and choose **Format Axis** from the shortcut menu. Click the **Scale** tab of the Format Axis dialog box.

2. Type a different unit for the **Major Unit**. Click the [OK] button to accept your changes and return to the chart.

Alter the Original Data

1. Select the worksheet or range that contains the charted data.

2. Click a cell that you want to alter or need to update. Type in the new data and press the (⏎Enter) key.

3. Click back to the chart to accept your changes and return to the chart.

See Also Cells, Format, Numbers, Workspace

CLIP ART

Clip art adds visual interest to your Excel worksheets. You can choose from numerous professionally prepared images.

Insert Clip Art

1. Choose **Insert**, **Picture**, **Clip Art** to open the Insert ClipArt dialog box.

2. Click the **Categories** of clip art in the **Pictures** tab and scroll through the options. At the bottom of the list of clip art is a **Keep Looking** link that allows you to view more clips.

3. Click the piece of clip art and choose **Insert Clip** from the pop-up menu, which inserts the clip art into your worksheet.

4. Click the **Close** ☒ button to close the Insert ClipArt dialog box.

See Also Borders, Drawing Tools

CLIPBOARD
see Copy and Cut   pgs 235-236

CLOSE

When you finish working in a workbook, you can close it and continue to work on other workbooks. You can close a file with or without saving changes.

Quick Tips		
Feature	*Button*	*Keyboard Shortcut*
Close Worksheet		Ctrl+F4 or Ctrl+W

Close a Workbook

1. Click the **Close Worksheet** ☒ button. If you changed the workbook, Excel asks you whether you want to save it.

2. Click the [Yes] button to save changes and close the worksheet. Click the [No] button to close the worksheet without saving changes. Click the [Cancel] button to return to working in your worksheet without closing it.

See Also Save Worksheets

COLOR
see Patterns   pg 246

COLUMNS

Columns are a vertical set of cells in a worksheet labeled with letters.

Quick Tips	
Feature	*Keyboard Shortcut*
Hide Columns	Ctrl + 0
Unhide Columns	Ctrl + ⬆Shift +)

Insert Columns

1. Select a cell near the column you want to add. The inserted column will be placed to the left of this cell.

2. Choose **Insert, Columns** to insert the column.

Delete Columns

1. Click the column heading of the column you want to delete.

2. Right-click and choose **Delete** from the shortcut menu.

Format Columns

1. Select a cell in the column you want to format.
2. Choose **Format, Column,** and select the appropriate option from the submenu.

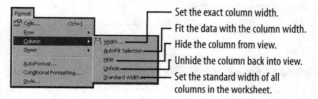

Set the exact column width.
Fit the data with the column width.
Hide the column from view.
Unhide the column back into view.
Set the standard width of all columns in the worksheet.

See Also Cells, Freezing Panes, Rows, Workspace

COMMENTS

When working in a workbook, you might find that you need to add a note reminding yourself to verify information when you work on the workbook later.

Insert Comments

1. Select the cell where you want to place a comment or place the cursor at the location where you want to insert a comment.
2. Choose **Insert, Comment** to open the comment text box.
3. Type the comment and click in the worksheet when finished. Notice that the cell's upper-right corner is now red to indicate the comment. Move the mouse pointer over the comment marker in the cell to view the comment in a ScreenTip.

View All Comments

Choose **View, Comments** to toggle between viewing all the worksheet comment text boxes.

Edit Comments

1. Right-click the commented cell and choose **Edit Comment** from the shortcut menu.

2. Type the changes into the comment text box and click in the worksheet when finished.

TIP

To delete a comment, right-click the comment and choose **Delete Comment** from the shortcut menu.

See Also Track Changes, Share and Protect Worksheets

CONDITIONAL FORMAT

At times, you might want the formatting of a cell to depend on the value it contains. Conditional Formatting lets you specify up to three conditions that, when met, cause the cell to be formatted in the manner defined for that condition. If none of the conditions are met, the cell keeps its original formatting.

Apply Conditional Formatting

1. Select the cells to which you want to apply conditional formatting.

2. Choose **Format, Conditional Formatting** to open the Conditional Formatting dialog box.

3. Click the **Condition 1** drop-down list to select whether the condition is for a cell value or formula. Click the operator that sets the condition. Type the value of the condition(s) to be met.

4. Click the [Format...] button to set the format to use when the condition is met. Click the options you want to set in the Format Cells dialog box. Click the [OK] button to accept your formatting conditions.

Indicate the type of operator.   Condition(s) to be met.

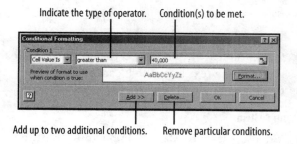

Add up to two additional conditions.   Remove particular conditions.

A
B
C

5. Click the ⬚ OK ⬚ button in the Conditional Formatting dialog box. Excel applies your formatting to any cells that meet the condition you specified.

See Also AutoFormat

COPY AND CUT

You can share information within and between workbooks in Excel by copying and cutting cells and objects. You can now copy and cut up to 12 different items onto the Clipboard at a time. The Clipboard is where items are stored before you paste them.

Quick Tips		
Feature	*Button*	*Keyboard Shortcut*
Copy	🖹	Ctrl + C or Ctrl + Insert
Copy Format		Ctrl + ⬆Shift + C
Copy Text Only		⬆Shift + F2
Cut	✂	Ctrl + X or ⬆Shift + Del

Copy

1. Select the cells or object you want to copy.
2. Click the **Copy** 🖹 button on the Standard toolbar. The original text remains in this location and a copy is placed on the Clipboard ready to be pasted.

A
B
C

Cut

1. Select the text or object you want to cut.
2. Click the **Cut** ✂ button on the Standard toolbar. This removes the text from the location and places it on the Clipboard ready to be pasted.

Copy Multiple Items

1. Choose **View, Toolbars, Clipboard** to open the Clipboard toolbar.
2. Select an item you want to copy and click the **Copy** 📋 button on the Clipboard toolbar after each time you select an item (up to 12). You can also use the original **Copy** 📋 and **Cut** ✂ buttons on the Standard toolbar to place items on the Clipboard toolbar.

Copy an item to the Clipboard.   Paste all items in the worksheet.

— Delete all items from the Clipboard.

Paste an item into the worksheet.

3. Move the mouse pointer over the Clipboard items and a ScreenTip displays what is contained in each copied clip (unless the clip is extensive, then only part of it displays). Click the clip to paste the item in the worksheet.

> **TIP**
>
> The Clipboard toolbar automatically appears when you click the **Cut** ✂ or **Copy** 📋 buttons multiple times. Click the **Close** ✖ button to close the Clipboard toolbar, or choose **View, Toolbars, Clipboard** to toggle the toolbar closed.

See Also Format Painter, Move Data, Objects, Paste

COUNT
see AutoCalculate   pg 231

CURRENCY
see Numbers   pg 244

DATA LISTS

You can use Excel for more than totaling numbers. You can also use the program as a simple data management program. You can keep track of clients, products, orders, expenses, and more. You can set up a data list and use some of Excel's data list features, including sorting, subtotaling, and filtering.

Set Up a Data List and Form

1. Type the headings for the columns of information. Select all the headers and format them. Format any other cells as necessary.

2. Select the cells where you want to establish the data list.

3. Choose **Data, Form**. This tells Excel that you want the selected cells to be used as the data labels. The form appears ready for you to enter data.

Enter Data with a Form

1. Choose **Data, Form** to open the data form for the worksheet data list.

2. Type the data for the first record into the data form while pressing the (Tab⇄) key between each field on the form.

3. Click the [New] button on the data list form. The data is automatically placed in your data list and the data form is ready for another entry.

4. Click the [Close] button on the form to return to working in your worksheet data list.

Apply and Check Data Validation

1. Click a cell anywhere in the data list field to which you want to apply data validation.

2. Choose **Data, Validation** to open the Data Validation dialog box.

3. Click an option from the **Allow** drop-down list of the **Validation criteria**.

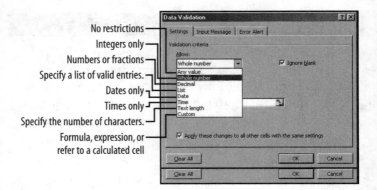

No restrictions
Integers only
Numbers or fractions
Specify a list of valid entries.
Dates only
Times only
Specify the number of characters.
Formula, expression, or refer to a calculated cell

4. Click any necessary operators from the **Data** drop-down list and type any restrictions for the final **Validation criteria**. Click the ⬚ OK button to accept your validation rules with Excel's default validation error message.

5. Type in a new data list record but add an incorrect entry in the validation field, then click the ⬚ New button. Click the ⬚ Retry button on the error message to return to the invalid record entry; type a correct entry and try clicking the ⬚ New button again. The record will be accepted.

Find a Record

1. Choose **Data, Form** to open the data form for the worksheet data list.

2. Click the ⬚ Criteria button. The form becomes blank awaiting your entry of the search criteria. Type in the search criteria and click the ⬚ Find Next button. Excel displays the first matching record. Continue clicking the ⬚ Find Next button until the record you want is displayed.

Modify a Record

1. Choose **Data, Form** to open the data form for the worksheet data list. Find the record you want to modify using the previous section steps.

2. Type the edits to the field and click the ⬚ Close button to accept the change and return to the worksheet data list.

Delete Data Records

1. Choose **Data, Form** to open the data form for the work-sheet data list. Find the record you want to modify using the previous section steps.

2. Click the ⬚ Delete ⬚ button to permanently remove the record from the data list. Click the ⬚ OK ⬚ button in the message box if you want to permanently delete the record from the data list; click the ⬚ Cancel ⬚ button if you don't want to delete the record.

Sort a Data List

1. Choose **Data, Sort** to open the Sort dialog box.

2. Click the field name from the **Sort by** drop-down list in **Ascending** or **Descending** order for the first sort criteria. Click any other field names from the **Then by** drop-down list in **Ascending** or **Descending** order for the second sort criteria.

3. Click the ⬚ OK ⬚ button and Excel sorts the entire data list.

Filter a Data List

1. Choose **Data, Filter, AutoFilter** to add drop-down arrows to each field header.

2. Click the arrow next to the field you want to use for the filtering criteria. Select what records you want to match. You can select a particular value, **Top 10**, **All**, **Custom,** or a specific record type in that field.

3. Click in the data list. Excel is already displaying only those records that meet the selected criteria. You can tell the database has been filtered because the filter arrow is a different color.

TIP

To remove an AutoFilter, choose **Data, Filter, AutoFilter**. The arrows disappear and the entire data list is again visible.

Add Record Subtotals

1. Sort the data on the field you want to subtotal.

2. Choose **Data**, **Subtotals** to open the Subtotal dialog box.

3. Click the **At Each Change In** drop-down list to select the specific column by which you want the subtotal grouped.

4. Click the **Use Function** drop-down list to select how you want the subtotaled rows to be calculated.

5. Click each **Add Subtotal To** option to indicate the column(s) on which you want the subtotal calculated.

6. Click the [OK] button. Excel inserts a subtotal row for each time the selected field changes, performs the selected function on the column you asked to total, and adds a grand total at the end of the data list.

See Also Filter Data, Sort Data

DIV/0!

see Error Messages   pg 237

DRAWING TOOLS

Excel provides many tools for you to draw and format shapes and text boxes in your worksheet.

Draw Shapes

1. Click the **Drawing** [icon] button on the Standard toolbar to open the Drawing toolbar.

2. Select the shape you want to draw in your worksheet: **Line** [icon], **Arrow** [icon], **Rectangle** [icon], or **Oval** [icon].

3. Click in the worksheet and drag the crosshatch pointer to the desired shape size.

Add Shape Color

1. Click the shape you want to color in your worksheet.

2. Click the appropriate button to select how you want to apply the color: **Fill Color** [icon] and **Line Color** [icon]. Click the desired color.

Alter Shape Style

1. Click the shape you want to style in your worksheet.

2. Click the appropriate button to select how you want to apply the style: **Line Style** ≣, **Dash Style** ≣, **Arrow Style** ≣, **Shadow** ▣, **3-D** ◻. Choose the desired style.

Insert AutoShapes

1. Click the [AutoShapes ▾] button and select the particular shape you want to add to your worksheet from the submenus.

2. Click in the worksheet and drag the crosshatch pointer to the desired shape size.

Rotate Shapes

1. Click the shape you want to rotate in your worksheet.

2. Click the **Free Rotate** ⟳ button on the Drawing toolbar.

3. Click the rotate pointer on the object rotate handles and drag the object to the desired rotation.

Add a Text Box

1. Click the **Text Box** ▤ button on the Drawing toolbar, or choose **Insert, Textbox**.

2. Click in the worksheet and drag the crosshatch pointer to the desired shape size.

3. Click the **Font Color** ▙ button and select the color for the font and type the information you want in the text box.

Add WordArt

1. Click the **WordArt** ▟ button on the Drawing toolbar.

2. Double-click a WordArt style in the WordArt Gallery dialog box and type the text in the Edit WordArt Text dialog box. Click the [OK] button to accept the changes and return to the worksheet.

See Also Clip Art, Objects

EMAIL

You can send the contents of the current Excel worksheet as the substance of the email message or as an attachment. Refer to the **Outlook** section for more information on email.

Send Workbook As an Email

1. Click the **Mail Recipient** 🗐 button on the Standard toolbar and if prompted, choose the option to **Send the Current Sheet As the Message Body** and click the ⬚ ᴏᴋ ⬚ button to continue.

2. Type the **To**, **Cc**, and any changes to the **Subject** line (should be the filename) and any other changes in the message. Click the ⬚ Send this Sheet ⬚ button and it will be sent.

TIP

Click the **Mail Recipient** 🗐 button again if you decide not to send the email and want to return to the workbook.

Send Workbook As an Email Attachment

1. Choose **File, Send To, Mail Recipient (as Attachment)**. This opens an email message and inserts the current workbook as an attachment.

2. Type the **To**, **Cc**, and any changes to the **Subject** line (should be the filename) and any other changes in the document. Click the ⬚ Send ▾ ⬚ button and the attachment is sent.

See Also Web Pages

ERROR MESSAGES

In Excel, a formula calculates a value based on the values in other cells of the workbook. Excel displays the result of a formula in a cell as a numeric value. When the result is an error, there are things you can do to correct it.

Fix the #### Error

When a cell contains **####**, the column is not wide enough to display the data. Click the column border and drag it to increase the size of the column width. The error disappears.

Fix the #DIV/0! Error

When a cell contains **#DIV/0!**, the formula is trying to divide a number by 0 or an empty cell. Retype the formula and press the ⏎Enter key. The error disappears.

Fix the #NAME? Error

When a cell contains **#NAME?**, the formula contains incorrectly spelled cell or function names. Retype the formula and press the ⏎Enter key. The error disappears.

Fix the #VALUE! Error

When a cell contains **#VALUE?**, the formula contains nonnumeric data or cell or function names that cannot be used in the calculation. Retype the formula and press the ⏎Enter key. The error disappears.

Recognize the #REF! Error

When a cell contains **#REF!**, the formula contains a reference to a cell that isn't valid. Frequently, this means you deleted a referenced cell. The best solution is to undo your action and review the cells involved in the formula.

Recognize Circular References

1. A circular reference results when one of the cells you are referencing in your calculation is the cell in which you want the calculation to appear.

2. Choose one of the following in the Microsoft Excel message box: the ⬜ OK button if you intend to create a circular reference, the ⬜ Cancel button if you want to edit and correct your formula, or the ⬜ Send this Sheet button if you want Excel to help you create and understand circular references.

See Also Spelling

FILTER DATA

In a large, columnar list of data, you may not want to see each and every row. Instead, you may want to work with just a set of rows. When you want to work with a subset of rows, you can filter the data. All the rows remain in the worksheet, but only those meeting the criteria you select are displayed.

Filter Data

1. Select the column titles for the data you want to filter.

2. Choose **Data, Filter, AutoFilter** to toggle between filtering columns and add drop-down arrows to each column title.

3. Click the arrow next to the column you want to use for the filtering criteria. Select what records you want to match. You can select a particular value, **Top 10, All, Custom,** or a specific record type in that field. Excel displays only those rows that meet the selected criteria.

See Also Data Lists, Sort Data

FIND DATA

You can use Excel's Find feature to locate data, text, characters, formatting, or even special characters.

Quick Tips		
Feature	*Button*	*Keyboard Shortcut*
Find	🔍	Ctrl+F or ⬆Shift+F4
Browse Next		Ctrl+PgDn
Browse Previous		Ctrl+PgUp
Repeat Find		⬆Shift+F4 or Ctrl+Alt+Y

Find Regular Data

1. Choose **Edit, Find** to open the Find dialog box.

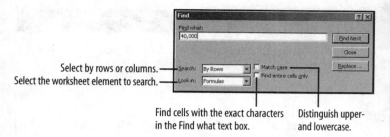

Select by rows or columns. — Find cells with the exact characters in the Find what text box.

Select the worksheet element to search. — Distinguish upper- and lowercase.

2. Type the text you want to locate in the **Find What** text box.

3. Click the [Find Next] button to move to each occurrence within the worksheet. If there aren't any to be found, Excel notifies you that it has finished searching the worksheet and that the item wasn't found.

See Also Replace Text

FLIP ROWS AND COLUMNS

Flipping rows and columns (transposing) is a special copy feature you might need to use if you want to change the layout of your worksheet.

Transpose Data

1. Select the range of cells you want to transpose. Click the **Copy** 📋 button.

2. Click the first cell in which you want to paste the range.

3. Choose **Edit, Paste Special** to open the Paste Special dialog box. Select the **Transpose** check box and click the [OK] button. The range is transposed (or flipped).

See Also Columns, Paste, Rows

FONTS

To draw attention to important data in a worksheet, you can change the text font options.

Quick Tips

Feature	Button	Keyboard Shortcut
Font		Ctrl+⇧Shift+F or Ctrl+D
Font Size		Ctrl+⇧Shift+P
Grow Font	A⃞	Ctrl+⇧Shift+.
Grow Font One Point		Ctrl+]
Hidden Text		Ctrl+⇧Shift+H
Shrink Font	A⃞	Ctrl+⇧Shift+,
Shrink Font One Point		Ctrl+[
Small Caps		Ctrl+⇧Shift+K
Subscript	x₂⃞	Ctrl+=
Superscript	x²⃞	Ctrl+⇧Shift+=
Symbol Font		Ctrl+⇧Shift+Q

Change Existing Fonts

1. Select the cells where you want to change the font.
2. Click the **Font** drop-down list on the Formatting toolbar and select the desired font.
3. Click the **Font Size** drop-down list on the Formatting toolbar and select the desired font size.
4. Click the **Font Color** drop-down list on the Formatting toolbar and select the desired font color.

Add Font Effects to Data

1. Select the cells to which you want to add a font effect.
2. Choose **Format, Cells; Font** tab.

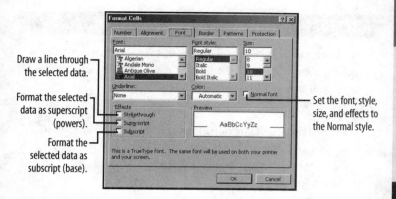

Draw a line through the selected data.

Format the selected data as superscript (powers).

Format the selected data as subscript (base).

Set the font, style, size, and effects to the Normal style.

D
E
F

3. Select from the various types of **Effects**. Click the
   [OK] button to accept the changes and return to the worksheet.

See Also Text

FORMAT

To draw attention to important data in a worksheet, you can format the data with any combination of bold, italic, and underline.

Quick Tips

Feature	Button	Keyboard Shortcut
Bold	**B**	Ctrl + B
Italic	*I*	Ctrl + I
Underline	U	Ctrl + U
Double Underline		Ctrl + ◆Shift + D
Strikethrough		Ctrl + 5

Format Bold, Italic, and Underline

1. Select the cells or text you want to format.
2. Click the **Bold** B button to add bold; **Italic** *I* to add italic; and **Underline** U to add underline to your data.

See Also Cells, Font, Format Painter

FORMAT PAINTER

You can use the Format Painter to copy the format from a selected object or cell and apply it to different objects or cells you select.

Copy Formats

1. Select the cells or object containing the format you want to copy and paste.

2. Click the **Format Painter** 🖌 button on the Standard toolbar.

3. Select the cells or object to which you want to apply the formatting; the items are formatted automatically.

Copy Formats to Multiple Locations

1. Select the cells or object containing the format you want to copy and paste. Double-click the **Format Painter** 🖌 button on the Standard toolbar.

2. Select each particular set of cells or objects to automatically apply the formatting. Click the **Format Painter** 🖌 button again when finished applying the format multiple places.

See Also Cells, Copy and Cut, Paste

FORMULAS

In Excel, a formula calculates a value based on the values in other cells of the workbook. Excel displays the result of a formula in a cell as a numeric value. Sometimes you don't want to use AutoSum because you have specific cell references on which you want to perform calculations. In this instance, you can type the desired formula directly into the cell.

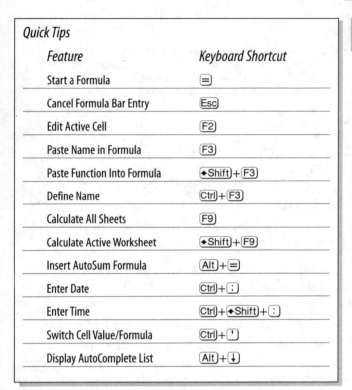

Quick Tips

Feature	Keyboard Shortcut
Start a Formula	⊟
Cancel Formula Bar Entry	Esc
Edit Active Cell	F2
Paste Name in Formula	F3
Paste Function Into Formula	⬆Shift + F3
Define Name	Ctrl + F3
Calculate All Sheets	F9
Calculate Active Worksheet	⬆Shift + F9
Insert AutoSum Formula	Alt + ⊟
Enter Date	Ctrl + ;
Enter Time	Ctrl + ⬆Shift + :
Switch Cell Value/Formula	Ctrl + '
Display AutoComplete List	Alt + ↓

D
E
F

Enter a Formula

1. Click the cell where you want the result of a formula to appear.

2. Type the equals ⊟ sign, the cell numbers, and the calculation for Excel to perform on the cells. The formula is displayed in the formula bar.

TIP

If you start to enter a formula and then decide you don't want to use it, you can skip entering the formula by pressing the Esc key.

TIP

Excel first performs any calculations within parentheses: (1+2)=3.
Then it performs multiplication or division calculations from left
to right: (12+24)/(3*2)=6. Finally, it performs any addition or sub-
traction from left to right: (12+24)/(3*2)-5=1.

Edit a Formula

1. Click the cell with the formula to make it the active cell.
   Notice that the formula is displayed in the formula bar.

2. Click the **Edit Formula** ▣ button and type or delete
   any changes to your formula.

3. Click the [OK] button. The changes are made and
   the result appears in the cell.

Copy a Formula

1. Click the cell that contains the formula you want to
   copy.

2. Click the **Copy** ▣ button on the Standard toolbar.

3. Click and drag the mouse pointer over all the cells
   where you want to paste the function. A line surrounds
   the cell you are copying.

4. Press the ⏎Enter key to paste the formula into each of
   the specified cells.

Name a Cell or Range

1. Select the cell or range of cells you want to name.

2. Choose **Insert, Name, Define** to open the Define
   Name dialog box, which displays the range coordinates
   and suggests a name.

3. Type the range name you want to use and click the
   [OK] button. Excel names the range. When the
   range is selected, it appears in the **Name** box.

Use a Name in a Formula

1. Click the cell where you want to enter a formula.

2. Type the formula to find a total using a named range
   and press the ⏎Enter key. Notice that the formula is displayed in the Formula bar.

> **TIP**
>
> If you forget the name of a range while you are typing a formula, choose **Insert**, **Name**, **Paste** and place the range name automatically in the formula.

See Also AutoCalculate, AutoSum, Cells, Functions

FREEZE PANES

Many times your worksheet will be large enough that you cannot view all the data onscreen at the same time. In addition, if you have added row or column titles, and you scroll down or to the right, some of the titles will be too far to the top or left of the worksheet for you to see. To help, you can freeze the heading rows and columns so that they are always visible.

Freeze Rows and Columns

1. Click in the cell to the right and below the area you want to freeze and choose **Window**, **Freeze Panes**.

2. Move through the worksheet (use the scrollbars) and notice that the rows and columns you selected are frozen so that you can reference data with the appropriate titles.

3. Choose **Window**, **Unfreeze Panes** to remove the freezing of columns and rows.

See Also Cells, Columns, Rows, Split Windows, Workspace

FUNCTIONS

Functions are abbreviated formulas that perform a specific operation on a group of values. Excel provides over 250 functions that can help you with tasks ranging from determining loan payments to calculating investment returns. First you type =**SUM**(in either lower- or uppercase letters. Then you select the range. You end the function by typing), which also tells Excel you are finished selecting the range.

Insert a Function

1. Click the cell in which the result of the function will appear.

2. Click the **Paste Function** 🔂 button on the Standard toolbar to open the Paste Function dialog box.

Calculate a loan payment based on constant payments and interest rates.

Return the argument's average.

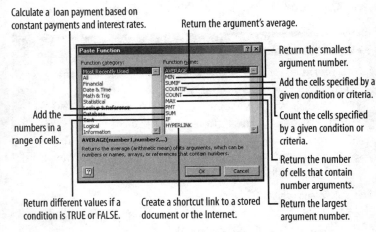

Return the smallest argument number.

Add the cells specified by a given condition or criteria.

Add the numbers in a range of cells.

Count the cells specified by a given condition or criteria.

Return the number of cells that contain number arguments.

Return different values if a condition is TRUE or FALSE.

Create a shortcut link to a stored document or the Internet.

Return the largest argument number.

3. Select the **Function Category** and scroll through the function names. Click the **Function Name** to review the function description at the bottom of the dialog box. Click the ⬛ OK ⬛ button when it is the function you want. Excel selects the obvious range of cells.

4. Type the cell range or range name and press the ⏎Enter key. Or, click the **Expand Dialog Box** 🔢 button, select the cell range, and click the **Decrease Dialog Box** 🔲 button. The calculated result appears in the active cell and the function is displayed in the Formula bar.

See Also AutoCalculate, AutoSum, Cells, Formulas

GO TO

The Go To command enables you to move quickly to any cell in a worksheet or workbook.

Quick Tips	
Feature	*Keyboard Shortcut*
Go To	Ctrl+G or F5

Use Go To

1. Choose **Edit, Go To** to open the Go To dialog box.
2. Type the cell reference and click the [OK] button. Excel moves to the selected cell.

See Also Find Data, Move Data, Replace Data

HEADER AND FOOTER

Headers and footers appear at the top and bottom of printed pages of Excel worksheets. Headers and footers can display the filename, date and time printed, worksheet name, page number, and more.

Insert Header and Footer

1. Choose **View, Header and Footer; Header and Footer** tab.
2. Click the **Header** drop-down list to see the various header options; or click the [Custom Header...] button to create your own header. Click the option you want to be in the left, center, and right section of the header.
3. Click the [Custom Footer...] button if you want to create your own footer; or click the **Footer** drop-down list and select from the options. Press the Tab key to move through the left, center, and right sections.

Insert number of total pages.   Insert time.

Change the font.   Insert active worksheet filename.

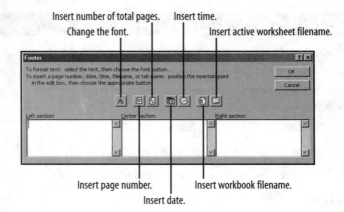

Insert page number.   Insert workbook filename.

Insert date.

4. Click the appropriate button to insert information into the footer section. Click the [OK] button to accept the footer text.

5. Click the [OK] button to accept the header and footer text. Click the **Print Preview** 🔍 button on the Standard toolbar to see how your worksheet previews.

See Also Page Setup, Print, Print Preview, Views

HYPERLINKS

When you click a hyperlink, the worksheet appears to *jump* to the related location. You can type a hyperlink directly into your worksheet or you can use the **Insert Hyperlink** 🔗 button on the Standard toolbar to manipulate the hyperlinks.

Quick Tips		
Feature	*Button*	*Keyboard Shortcut*
Insert Hyperlink	🔗	Ctrl + K

Type a URL Hyperlink Into a Worksheet

1. Click the cell(s) in the worksheet where you want to add the hyperlink.

2. Type the URL into your worksheet and the address automatically becomes a hyperlink.

3. Move the mouse pointer over the hyperlink and the location displays in a ScreenTip.

Insert a Hyperlink

1. Select the cells that you want to make into a hyperlink.

2. Click the **Insert Hyperlink** 🔳 button on the Standard toolbar to open the Insert Hyperlink dialog box.

3. Type the link into the **Type the File or Web Page Name** text box or select from the recent files, browsed pages, or inserted links list. Click the ⬜ OK ⬜ button to accept the changes and return to the worksheet.

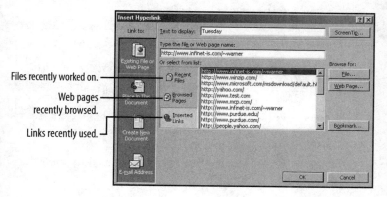

Files recently worked on.

Web pages recently browsed.

Links recently used.

TIP

To delete a hyperlink, right-click the hyperlink and choose **Hyperlink, Remove Hyperlink**. To edit a hyperlink, right-click the hyperlink and choose **Hyperlink, Edit Hyperlink**. Make the changes and click the ⬜ OK ⬜ button.

See Also Objects, Text, Save Worksheets, Web Pages

ITALIC
see Format   pg 239

JUSTIFICATION
see Alignment   pg 231

LANDSCAPE
see Page Setup   pg 245

LINK OBJECTS
see Charts   pg 232

MACROS

You can create a macro that will accomplish just about any task. With the macro recording option, you can record your actions and then these actions will be performed for you when you run the macro.

Quick Tips		
Feature	*Button*	*Keyboard Shortcut*
Macro	▶	(Alt)+(F8)

Create a Macro

1. Choose **Tools, Macro, Record New Macro** to open the Record Macro dialog box.

2. Type a name in the **Macro Name** text box.

3. Click the [OK] button. The Macro toolbar appears with the **Stop Recording** ■ and **Pause Recording** ⏸ buttons.

4. Perform any tasks that you want the macro to record and click the **Stop Recording** ■ button when finished.

Run a Macro

1. Press the (Alt)+(F8) keys to open the Macros dialog box.

2. Double-click the **Macro Name** and the macro runs.

> **TIP**
>
> To delete a macro, press (Alt)+(F8) to open the Macro dialog box. Click the macro name and click the [Delete] button. Excel asks if you want to delete the macro. Click the [Yes] button to delete the macro. Click the [Cancel] button to return to your worksheet.

See Also Find Text, Replace Text

MARGINS
see Page Setup   pg 245

MOVE CELLS

You can reorganize cells in an Excel worksheet by moving items as you work. This method can be faster than cutting and pasting text.

Quick Tips

Feature	Keyboard Shortcut
Move Data	(F2)

M
N
O

Move Cells to a New Location

1. Select the cells you want to move.

2. Press and hold down the left mouse button on the border of the selected cells and drag the pointer to the new location.

3. Release the mouse button to drop the cells in the new location.

See Also Copy and Cut, Objects, Paste

#NAME?
see Error Messages   pg 237

NEW WORKBOOK

Excel presents a new blank workbook each time you start the application. You can create another new workbook at any time.

Quick Tips		
Feature	Button	Keyboard Shortcut
New Workbook	☐	Ctrl + N
Insert New Worksheet		⬆Shift + F11 or
		Alt + ⬆Shift + F1

Create a New Workbook

Click the **New** ☐ button on the Standard toolbar and Excel opens a new workbook.

Use a New Workbook Spreadsheet Solution

1. Choose **File**, **New** to open the New dialog box. Select the tab that corresponds with what you want to create.

2. Double-click either the worksheet to begin inserting the new text or the spreadsheet solution sample, filling in information as necessary.

See Also Open Workbook, Worksheets

NUMBERS

You can apply different styles to cells, depending on the type of data the cells contain. Using styles affects the way cells display data but does not limit the type of data you can enter.

Quick Tips

Feature	Button	Keyboard Shortcut
Format Style		`Alt`+`'`
Format Cells		`Ctrl`+`1`
General Number Format		`Ctrl`+`Shift`+`~`
Currency Format	`$`	`Ctrl`+`Shift`+`$`
Percentage Format	`%`	`Ctrl`+`Shift`+`%`
Exponential Format		`Ctrl`+`Shift`+`^`
Date Format		`Ctrl`+`Shift`+`#`
Time Format		`Ctrl`+`Shift`+`@`
Number Format		`Ctrl`+`Shift`+`!`

Apply Styles to Numeric Data

1. Select the cells you want to format.
2. Click the **Increase Decimal** or **Decrease Decimal** buttons on the Formatting toolbar to increase or decrease the number of decimal places.
3. Click the **Comma Style** button on the Formatting toolbar to apply commas to numbers.
4. Click the **Percent Style** button on the Formatting toolbar to apply percentages to numbers.
5. Click the **Currency Style** button on the Formatting toolbar to apply the currency style to numbers.

Change Cell Number Format

1. Select the cells you want to format.
2. Choose **Format, Cells**; **Number** tab.

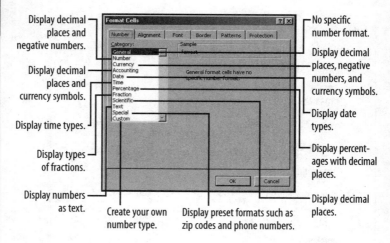

Display decimal places and negative numbers.

Display decimal places and currency symbols.

Display time types.

Display types of fractions.

Display numbers as text.

Create your own number type.

Display preset formats such as zip codes and phone numbers.

No specific number format.

Display decimal places, negative numbers, and currency symbols.

Display date types.

Display percentages with decimal places.

Display decimal places.

3. Click the **Category** option and click the `OK` button to accept the changes and return to the worksheet.

See Also Cells, Fonts

OBJECTS

An Excel object can be any of numerous types of elements that you add to your worksheet: file, art, chart, worksheet, photo, movie, text clip, and so on.

Insert a New Object

1. Choose **Insert, Object; Create New** tab.

2. Click the **Object Type** from the list box. Click the `OK` button to accept the changes and return to the worksheet.

3. Click directly on the object and make any changes to it using the associated toolbar.

Insert an Object File

1. Choose **Insert, Object; Create from File** tab.

2. Type in the **File Name** or click the `Browse...` button to select the file from a specific location.

3. Select the **Link to File** option if you want the object to be linked to this worksheet and the source file. This means that any changes you make in the source file will be reflected in your worksheet. Click the [OK] button to accept the changes and return to the worksheet.

Resize Objects

1. Click once directly on an object and handles appear on all sides and corners of the object.
2. Move the mouse pointer over one of the handles; click and hold the handle after the pointer becomes a two-headed arrow.
3. Drag the handle to the desired size. If you drag from the corner handles, the height and width increase or decrease proportionately. If you drag from the side handles, only the height or width increases or decreases. Click elsewhere in the worksheet to deselect the object.

Move Objects

1. Click once directly on an object and handles appear on all sides and corners of the object.
2. Move the mouse pointer over the object, click and hold the pointer when the pointer appears with a gray box below it. Drag the object to the new location and drop the object.

Delete Objects

1. Click once directly on an object and handles appear on all sides and corners of the object.
2. Press the [Del] key and the object is removed from the worksheet.

> **TIP**
> If you link an object in your worksheet, you can quickly edit or open the source file by double-clicking the object. You can also copy, cut, and paste an object to a different location.

See Also Clip Art, Drawing Tools, Excel Worksheets

OPEN WORKBOOK

Each time you want to work with a workbook, you need to open it using the Open dialog box.

Quick Tips

Feature	*Button*	*Keyboard Shortcut*
Open Workbook	🖼	Ctrl+O or Ctrl+F12 or Ctrl+Alt+F2

Open a Workbook

1. Click the **Open** 🖼 button on the Standard toolbar to display the Open dialog box listing the saved Excel workbooks.

2. Click the **Places Bar** option for the location of the file you want to open.

3. Click the **Look In** drop-down list to help locate the correct file or drive. You can also click the **Up One Folder** 🔼 button to move through folders.

4. Double-click the file you want to open and Excel opens the workbook.

Open Files of Different Type

1. Click the **Open** 🖼 button on the Standard toolbar to open the Open dialog box listing the saved Excel workbooks.

2. Click the **Files of Type** drop-down list and select the file type. The Open dialog box displays only files that are of the type you selected.

3. Double-click the file you want to open and Excel opens the workbook. If the file cannot be opened because of a type mismatch, Excel alerts you of this with a message box.

See Also New Workbook, Save Workbook

ORIENTATION
see Page Setup   pg 245

PAGE SETUP

You can adjust the page orientation, scaling, paper size, and margins for worksheets.

Set Margins

1. Choose **File, Page Setup; Margins** tab.

2. Type in or use the spin box controls to set the **Top, Bottom, Left, Right** margins, and **Header** and **Footer** sizes from the edge.

3. Click the ⬚ ok ⬚ button to accept the changes and return to the worksheet.

Change from Portrait to Landscape

1. Choose **File, Page Setup; Page** tab.

2. Select the **Orientation** of **Portrait** or **Landscape**. Click the ⬚ ok ⬚ button to accept the changes and return to the worksheet.

Select the Paper Size

1. Choose **File, Page Setup; Page** tab.

2. Select the **Paper Size** from the drop-down list. Click the ⬚ ok ⬚ button to accept the changes and return to the worksheet.

Select the Page Scale

1. Choose **File, Page Setup; Page** tab.

2. Select the percentage you want the page to **Adjust to % Normal Size** or adjust the spin box controls to **Fit to Page(s) Wide By Tall**. Click the ⬚ ok ⬚ button to accept the changes and return to the worksheet.

See Also Alignment, Columns, Print, Print Area, Print Preview

PASTE

You can share information within and between worksheets in Excel by pasting cells and objects. You can now paste up to 12 different items from the Clipboard at a time. The Clipboard is where items are stored after you copy or cut them.

Quick Tips		
Feature	Button	Keyboard Shortcut
Paste	📋	Ctrl+V or ⇧Shift+Insert
Paste Format		Ctrl+⇧Shift+V
Paste Function Into Formula		⇧Shift+F3

Paste Text or Objects

1. Place the cursor in the location where you want to paste the cells or object. You must have already cut or copied cells or an object in order for the **Paste** 📋 button to be active.

2. Click the **Paste** 📋 button on the Standard toolbar.

Paste Multiple Items

1. Choose **View, Toolbars, Clipboard** to open the Clipboard toolbar. You must have already cut or copied cells or an object for there to be any items on the Clipboard.

2. Place the cursor in the location where you want to paste a clip item.

Paste all items in the worksheet. Delete all items from the Clipboard.

Copy an item to the Clipboard. Paste an item into the worksheet.

3. Move the mouse pointer over the Clipboard items and a ScreenTip displays what is contained in each clip (unless the clip is extensive, then only part of it will display).

4. Click the clip art that you want to paste. When finished, click the **Close** ☒ button to close the Clipboard toolbar, or choose **View**, **Toolbars**, **Clipboard** to toggle the toolbar closed.

Paste Special

1. Place the cursor in the location where you want to paste the cells or object. You must have already cut or copied cells or an object.

2. Choose **Edit**, **Paste Special** to open the Paste Special dialog box.

3. Select the **Paste** option to paste the item; select **Paste Link** to create a shortcut link to the source file (any changes you make to the source file will automatically be reflected in your worksheet). The **Paste Link** option won't be available if your copied selection isn't linkable.

4. Select the **As** option for how you want to paste the item. The **Result** area of the dialog box explains each type of paste. Click the ▭ OK ▭ button to accept the changes and return to the worksheet.

See Also Copy and Cut, Hyperlink, Move Cells, Replace Data

P
Q
R

PATTERNS

You can apply colors and patterns to the background of selected cells.

Apply Cell Shading

1. Select the cells you want to shade.

2. Choose **Format**, **Cells**; **Patterns** tab.

3. Select a **Color** and click the **Pattern** drop-down list to apply a pattern to the background of the cell. Click the ▭ OK ▭ button to accept the changes and return to the worksheet.

TIP

You can also click a color from the **Fill Color** drop-down palette on the Formatting toolbar to apply only a cell color.

See Also Borders, Cells, Fonts

PIVOTTABLES AND PIVOTCHARTS

Pivot tables are interactive reports that summarize and analyze Excel worksheet data or an external database. You can alter your data analysis without creating a new report each time. A pivot table cross-tabulates data in columns and rows and allows you to filter and sort the display data as well as expand the field details.

Create a PivotTable and a PivotChart Report

1. Select a cell in the table that you want to serve as the foundation for the pivot table (usually column headers).

2. Choose **Data, PivotTable and PivotChart Report** to open the PivotTable and PivotChart Wizard.

3. Select the **Microsoft Excel List or Database** option for the data that you want to analyze and choose whether you want to create a **PivotTable** or **PivotChart** report, then choose the [Next >] button. Excel automatically selects the range of cells for the pivot table, but allows you to change it in the second step of the wizard.

4. Verify or reselect the range of cells (there must be more than one row selected), then choose the [Next >] button.

5. Select where you want to place the pivot table, either in a **New Worksheet** or the **Existing Worksheet**. Also select from the optional buttons to format or alter your settings, then choose the [Finish] button.

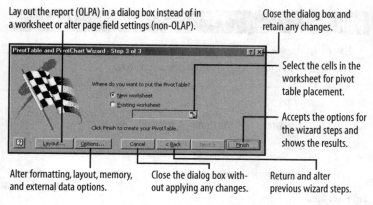

Lay out the report (OLPA) in a dialog box instead of in a worksheet or alter page field settings (non-OLAP).

Close the dialog box and retain any changes.

Select the cells in the worksheet for pivot table placement.

Accepts the options for the wizard steps and shows the results.

Alter formatting, layout, memory, and external data options.

Close the dialog box without applying any changes.

Return and alter previous wizard steps.

6. Click the particular field you want to summarize on the PivotTable toolbar and drag it into the **Data** area. Click and drag the fields you want on the **Page** and in **Rows** and **Columns**. You can move these fields back and forth if you select one in error.

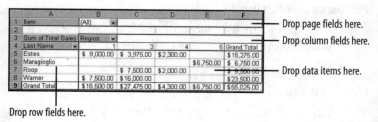

Drop page fields here.

Drop column fields here.

Drop data items here.

Drop row fields here.

7. Click the **Chart Wizard** 📊 button on the PivotTable toolbar to create a new chart sheet based on the pivot table you just created. You can move the fields around in the chart using the PivotTable toolbar. If you closed the toolbar, choose **View**, **Toolbars**, **PivotTable** to display it.

See Also Charts, Data Lists

PORTRAIT
see Page Setup   pg 245

138

PRINT

Excel makes it easy to print a worksheet and enables you to select the printer and worksheet settings.

Quick Tips

Feature	Button	Keyboard Shortcut
Print	🖨	Ctrl+P or Ctrl+⬆Shift+F12

Set Print Area

1. Select the cells you want to print.

2. Choose **File, Print Area, Set Print Area**; repeat this if you need to reset the area. You can select **Clear Print Area** if you need to remove the set print area.

Print Current Worksheet Defaults

Click the **Print** 🖨 button on the standard toolbar; the worksheet prints according to the settings in your page setup.

Enter Print Options

1. Choose **File, Print** to open the Print dialog box.

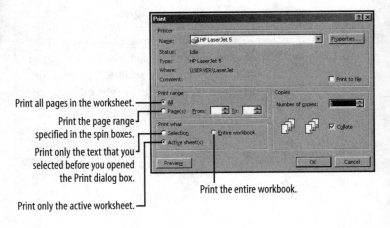

Print all pages in the worksheet.

Print the page range specified in the spin boxes.

Print only the text that you selected before you opened the Print dialog box.

Print only the active worksheet.

Print the entire workbook.

2. Select the **Page Range** that you want as your print job. Select the **Number of Copies** you want printed and whether you want Excel to **Collate** a multiple page worksheet. Click the ⬚OK⬚ button to send the print job to the printer.

Print Column or Row Titles

1. Choose **File, Page Setup; Sheet** tab.

2. Click the **Expand Dialog Box** 🔣 button in the **Rows to Repeat At Top** text box and drag directly in your worksheet to select the rows you want to repeat on multiple printed pages. Click the **Resize Dialog** button to return to the full Page Setup dialog box.

3. Click the **Expand Dialog Box** 🔣 button in the **Columns to Repeat At Left** text box and drag directly in your worksheet to select the columns you want to repeat on multiple printed pages. Click the **Decrease Dialog Box** 🔣 button to return to the full Page Setup dialog box.

4. Click the ⬚OK⬚ button to accept the changes and return to the worksheet.

Print Gridlines and Sheet Options

1. Choose **File, Page Setup; Sheet** tab.

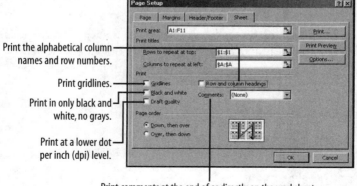

Print the alphabetical column names and row numbers.

Print gridlines.

Print in only black and white, no grays.

Print at a lower dot per inch (dpi) level.

Print comments at the end of or directly on the worksheet.

2. Select from the various **Print** options. Click the ⬚ OK ⬚ button to accept the changes and return to the worksheet.

Choose a Different Printer

1. Choose **File**, **Print** to open the Print dialog box.
2. Click the **Name** drop-down list and select the printer you want to print to.

See Also Page Setup, Print Preview

PRINT PREVIEW

Print Preview enables you to see worksheet pages onscreen as they will appear printed on paper, displaying page numbers, headers, footers, fonts, orientation, columns and rows, gridlines, and margins.

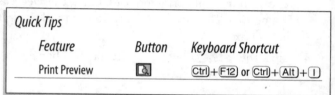

Quick Tips		
Feature	Button	Keyboard Shortcut
Print Preview	🔍	Ctrl+F12 or Ctrl+Alt+I

Preview a Worksheet

P
Q
R

1. Click the **Print Preview** 🔍 button on the Standard toolbar.
2. Click directly on the previewed worksheet and the magnification increases. Click directly on the previewed worksheet again and the magnification returns to the original percentage.
3. Click the ⬚ Close ⬚ button on the Print Preview toolbar to return to the worksheet.

See Also Page Setup, Print, Views, Workspace .

PRINT LAYOUT VIEW
see Views   pg 253

PROTECT WORKBOOKS

When you share files with other users, you might find it useful to protect your workbooks. You can protect your workbooks by restricting access to the workbook and preventing changes from being made within each particular workbook.

Protect Sheet

1. Choose **Tools, Protection, Protect Sheet**.

2. Select the protection options from the **Protect Worksheet For** list. **Contents** prevents changes to cells and chart items. **Objects** prevents editing, moving, deleting, or resizing of objects in worksheets and chart sheets. **Scenarios** prevents changes to worksheet scenario definitions.

3. Type a password in the **Password (optional)** text box and press the ⏎Enter key. This means that any other user will need to enter this password to open this workbook. Type the same password in the Confirm Password dialog box and press the ⏎Enter key. (If asked to save the workbook, choose ⬚ OK ⬚.)

4. Click the ⬚ OK ⬚ button to accept the changes and return to the worksheet. Have someone else try to open the file with and without the password.

Protect Workbook

1. Choose **Tools, Protection, Protect Workbook**.

2. Select the options from the **Protect Workbook For** list. **Structure** protects worksheets from being added, deleted, moved, hidden, unhidden, or renamed. **Windows** protects the workbook windows from being moved, closed, resized, hidden, or unhidden.

3. Type a password in the **Password (optional)** text box and press the ⏎Enter key. This means that any other user will need to enter this password to open this workbook. Type the same password in the Confirm Password dialog box and press the ⏎Enter key. (If asked to save the workbook, choose ⬚ OK ⬚.)

4. Click the ▭ OK ▭ button to accept the changes and return to the worksheet. Have someone else try to open the file with and without the password.

Protect Shared Workbook

1. Choose **Tools, Protection, Protect and Share Workbook**.

2. Select that you want to **Protect Workbook For Sharing With Track Changes**. You will be able to share the workbook, but any changes other users make will be tracked.

3. Type a password in the **Password (optional)** text box and press the ⏎Enter key. This means that any other user will need to enter this password to open this workbook. Type the same password in the Confirm Password dialog box and press the ⏎Enter key. (If asked to save the workbook, choose ▭ OK ▭.)

4. Click the ▭ OK ▭ button to accept the changes and return to the worksheet. Have someone else try to open the file with and without the password.

See Also Comments, Share Workbooks, Track Changes

REDO
see Undo   pg 252

#REF!
see Error Messages   pg 237

REPLACE DATA

You can quickly replace numbers, text, data formats, and special characters in Excel.

Quick Tips	
Feature	*Keyboard Shortcut*
Replace	Ctrl+H

Search and Replace Data

1. Choose **Edit, Replace** to open the Find and Replace dialog box.

2. Type the text you want to locate in the **Find What** text box. Any text from a previous search will still be in the dialog box, unless you have exited Excel.

3. Click in the **Replace With** text box (or press the Tab⇆ key) and type the text you want to replace it with.

4. Select from the Search options and click the appropriate action button.

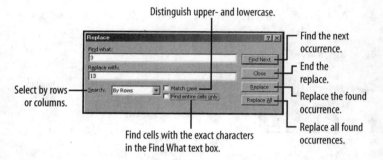

Distinguish upper- and lowercase.

Find the next occurrence.

End the replace.

Replace the found occurrence.

Replace all found occurrences.

Select by rows or columns.

Find cells with the exact characters in the Find What text box.

See Also Copy and Cut, Find Data, Move Data, Paste, Redo and Undo

ROWS

Rows are a horizontal set of cells in a worksheet labeled with numbers.

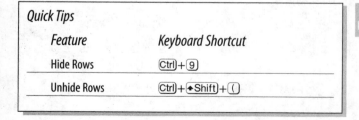

Quick Tips

Feature	Keyboard Shortcut
Hide Rows	Ctrl + 9
Unhide Rows	Ctrl + ⇧Shift + (

P
Q
R

Insert Rows

1. Select a row or cell where you want to add a row.

2. Choose **Insert, Rows** to insert the row above the original cell or row selection.

Delete Rows

1. Click the row heading of the row you want to delete.

2. Right-click and choose **Delete** from the shortcut menu.

Format Rows

1. Select a cell in the row you want to format.

2. Choose **Format, Row,** and select the appropriate option from the submenu.

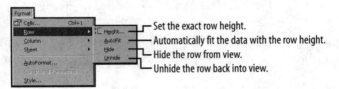

— Set the exact row height.
— Automatically fit the data with the row height.
— Hide the row from view.
— Unhide the row back into view.

See Also Cells, Columns, Freezing Panes, Workspace

SAVE WORKBOOKS

Save the workbook you are working in to store it on disk. A good practice is to save your workbooks frequently as you work in them.

Quick Tips		
Feature	*Button*	*Keyboard Shortcut*
Save	🖫	Ctrl+S or Shift+F12 or Alt+Shift+F2
Save As		F12 or Alt+F2

Save a Worksheet

1. Click the **Save** 🔲 button on the Standard toolbar and the workbook saves any recent changes. If you haven't saved the workbook yet, the Save As dialog box appears.

2. Click the **Places Bar** option for the location of the file you want to save. Click the **Save In** drop-down list to help locate the correct folder or drive. You can also click the **Up One Folder** 🔳 button to move through folders.

3. Type the **File Name** and click the 🔲 Save button.

Save As a Different Name

1. Choose **File, Save As** to open the Save As dialog box.

2. Click the **Places Bar** button for the location of the file you want to save. Click the **Save In** drop-down list to help locate the correct folder or drive. You can also click the **Up One Folder** 🔳 button to move through folders.

3. Type the new **File Name** and click the 🔲 Save button.

Save As a Different File Type

1. Choose **File, Save As** to open the Save As dialog box.

2. Click the **Places Bar** button for the location of the file you want to save. Click the **Save In** drop-down list to help locate the correct folder or drive. You can also click the **Up One Folder** 🔳 button to move through folders.

3. Click the **Save As Type** drop-down list and select the desired file type. Type the **File Name** and click the 🔲 Save button.

See Also Close Workbooks, Open Workbooks, Worksheets

SEARCH
see Find   pg 239

SHADING
see Patterns   pg 246

SHARE WORKBOOKS

You can share workbooks either by restricting access to the worksheet or preventing changes from being made within each particular worksheet.

Set File Share Options

1. Choose **Tools, Share Workbook** to open the Share Workbook dialog box.

2. Select whether you want to **Allow Changes By More Than One User At the Same Time**. This will save the workbook as a shared workbook. Click the ⬚ OK ⬚ button to accept the changes and return to the worksheet.

See Also Comments, Protect Workbooks, Track Changes

SPELLING

You can check spelling in Excel 2000 quickly and easily. Of course, you should always review your workbooks, but it never hurts to have a little help.

Quick Tips		
Feature	*Button*	*Keyboard Shortcut*
Spelling	🔡	F7
Next Misspelling		Alt + F7

Check Spelling

1. Click the **Spelling** 🔡 button on the Standard toolbar. The Spelling dialog box opens, displaying the first spelling error it finds.

2. Click the appropriate spelling option in the **Suggestions** list box; if one doesn't work, type the change directly in the **Change to** text box.

3. Click the appropriate button to make the selected **Suggestions** change.

A word that shouldn't be altered
and it should not flag any other
instances of the word.

A word that shouldn't be altered.

Make the
selected
Suggestions
change.

Add a word to
the dictionary
so that it will
remember the
word as correct
in the future.

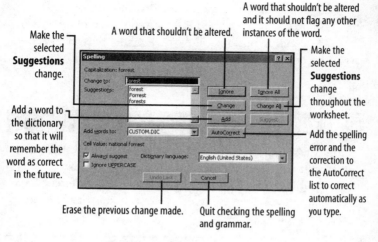

Make the
selected
Suggestions
change
throughout the
worksheet.

Add the spelling
error and the
correction to
the AutoCorrect
list to correct
automatically as
you type.

Erase the previous change made.   Quit checking the spelling   you type.
and grammar.

4. Click the [Yes] or [No] button if Excel asks you to
continue checking the worksheet, especially if you didn't
start checking at the beginning of the worksheet.

5. Click the [OK] button if Excel displays a message
telling you the spelling check is complete. This means
all inaccuracies have been reviewed.

See Also Error Messages

SORT DATA

You can arrange the information in your worksheets by
sorting rows and columns alphabetically, numerically, or
by date.

Sort Data

1. Choose **Data, Sort** to open the Sort dialog box. Excel
automatically selects the logical cells in your worksheet
or you can preselect them.

2. Select the **My List Has** option depending on whether
you have a **Header Row** or **No Header Row**.

3. Click the **Sort By** drop-down list to select the first column to sort and the corresponding **Ascending** or
Descending option. If you have more than one column

to sort by in a sequence, click one or both of the **Then By** drop-down lists and indicate the **Ascending** or **Descending** option. Click the ▭ ᴏᴋ ▭ button to accept the changes and review the sorted data.

See Also Data Lists, Filter Data

SPLIT WINDOW

You can simultaneously view two parts of a worksheet if you split the window into multiple panes. This is convenient when you need to view information at different locations in a worksheet in order to work in another portion of the worksheet.

Quick Tips	
Feature	*Keyboard Shortcut*
Close Split Pane	(Alt)+(⬆Shift)+(C)
Split Worksheet	(Alt)+(Ctrl)+(S)
Other Pane	(F6) or (⬆Shift)+(F6)

Split the Worksheet View

1. Choose **Window, Split** and click in the worksheet where you want to view the split area. You can click and drag the split bar at any time.

2. Move through each split with the scrollbars to position the worksheet view areas.

3. Double-click each split bar to remove the split, or choose **Window, Remove Split**.

See Also View Multiple Worksheets, Views, Workspace

TRACK CHANGES

Sometimes you find that you have to make corrections in a worksheet, or perhaps you are working on a report in a team environment. To determine who made what changes when, you can track the changes onscreen with revision marks.

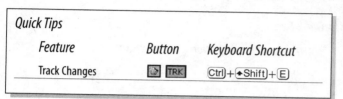

Quick Tips

Feature	Button	Keyboard Shortcut
Track Changes	📋 TRK	Ctrl + ⬆Shift + E

Track Worksheet Changes

1. Choose **Tools, Track Changes, Highlight Changes** to open the Highlight Changes dialog box.
2. Select from the available tracking options.

Turns on workbook sharing and tracks changes. ⎯
Change the time that you want to display changes. ⎯
Select whose changes are highlighted. ⎯
Select a specific range of cells to highlight changes. ⎯

Show highlighted changes onscreen. ⎯
Display changes in a history worksheet. ⎯

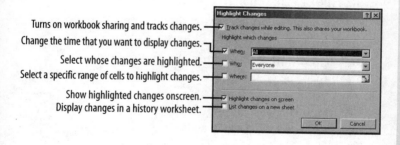

3. Click the ⬚OK⬚ button to accept the changes and return to the worksheet.

See Also Accept and Reject Changes

UNDERLINE
see Format   pg 239

UNDO AND REDO

Undo and Redo are convenient when you want to see how your worksheet looks with and without changes you make. In addition, this can be convenient when you have made an error in your worksheet.

Quick Tips

Feature	Button	Keyboard Shortcut
Undo	↶	Ctrl+Z or Alt+←Backspace
Redo or Repeat	↷	Ctrl+Y or Alt+←Shift+←Backspace or F4 or Alt+↵Enter

Use Undo and Redo

1. Type or make change(s) in your worksheet.
2. Click the **Undo** ↶ button as many times as necessary to undo the change(s).
3. Click the **Redo** ↷ button as many times as necessary to redo the change(s).

> **TIP**
>
> You can also click the **Undo** or **Redo** drop-down list arrows to select the exact changes you want to make.

See Also Close Worksheets, Save Worksheets

VIEW MULTIPLE WORKSHEETS

If you don't want to constantly switch between worksheets, you can view multiple Excel worksheets onscreen. The worksheet displaying a darker title bar is considered the active worksheet; when you type, text goes there.

View Multiple Worksheets

1. Open all the worksheets you want to simultaneously view.

2. Choose **Window, Arrange All**.

3. Click the title bar or click in the body of the worksheet where you want to work.

TIP

To return to viewing only one entire worksheet, double-click the title bar of the worksheet in which you want to work.

See Also Open Worksheets, Split Windows, Workspace

WEB PAGES

You can view your worksheets as Web pages in Web Page Preview even before you have saved the file as a Web page.

Quick Tips

Feature	*Keyboard Shortcut*
Web Go Back	Alt + ←
Web Go Forward	Alt + →

Use Web Page Preview

Choose, **File, Web Page Preview** to open the Internet Explorer browser and display the worksheet. Click the **Close** ☒ button to return to the Excel worksheet.

Save As a Web Page

1. Choose **File, Save As Web Page** to open the Save As dialog box.

2. Click the **Places Bar** option for the location of the file you want to save. Click the **Save In** drop-down list to help locate the correct folder or drive. You can also click the **Up One Folder** button to move through folders.

3. Click the **Selection: Sheet** option if you want to save only the current worksheet as a Web page. The **Add Interactivity** check box becomes available; click this option if you want to be able to enter and calculate data on the Web. Click the `Change Title...` button and type in a **Page Title** if you want the page title to be different than the filename, and click the `OK` button. Note that the `Publish` button allows you to select each of these options in one main Publish as a Web Page dialog box.

4. Type the **File Name** and click the `Save` button.

See Also Email, Save Workbooks, Workspace

WORKSHEETS

A new workbook includes three sheets by default. You can easily name, add, delete, and copy worksheets.

> **Quick Tips**
>
> | Feature | Keyboard Shortcut |
> | --- | --- |
> | Insert New Worksheet | ⬆Shift + F11 or Alt + ⬆Shift + F1 |
> | Insert Chart Sheet | Alt + F1 |

Name Worksheets

1. Double-click the sheet tab of the sheet you want to rename; the current name is highlighted.

2. Type the new name and press the ↵Enter key. Excel displays the new name on the worksheet tab.

Insert a Worksheet

1. Click the worksheet in which you want to insert the new worksheet *before* it.

2. Choose **Insert, Worksheet**. Excel inserts a new blank worksheet. This new worksheet is selected.

Delete a Worksheet

1. Click the sheet you want to delete.

2. Choose **Edit, Delete Sheet**.

3. Click the [OK] button to confirm the deletion. The worksheet and all its data will be deleted. You cannot undo the action of deleting a worksheet. Make sure you have a backup copy of the workbook or are positive that you will never need the worksheet again.

Copy a Worksheet to Another Workbook

1. Open the workbooks you want to copy from and copy to. Click the worksheet tab you want to copy.

2. Choose **Edit, Move or Copy Sheet** to open the Move or Copy dialog box.

3. Click the **To Book** drop-down list and select the workbook you want to move it to. Select the tab order location you want to place the copy of the worksheet.

4. Click the **Create a Copy** check box. Click the [OK] button; the worksheet is copied.

See Also Open Workbooks, Save Workbooks, Workspace

WORKSPACE

You can click the scrollbars to move the view of the worksheet. Press the keys on the keyboard to move the cursor through the worksheet or view the rulers or full screen.

Quick Tips

Feature	Button	Keyboard Shortcut
End Row Left		Ctrl + ←
End Row Right		Ctrl + →
End Column Up		Ctrl + ↑
End Column Down		Ctrl + ↓
Browse Selection		Alt + Ctrl + Home
Minimize Workbook Window	▬	Ctrl + F9
Maximize Workbook Window	▢	Ctrl + F10
Move Workbook Window		Ctrl + F7
Restore Workbook Window	▣	Ctrl + F5
Size Workbook Window		Ctrl + F8

Use Scrollbar Options

Click on the **Up** and **Down** scrollbar arrows to scroll through the worksheet. Click directly on the large scrollbar and drag it up and down to quickly move through the worksheet.

Increase Worksheet View Size

1. Click the **Zoom** drop-down list on the Standard toolbar.

2. Select the percentage or descriptive size you want to view your worksheet in. You can also click directly on the **Zoom** list box and type in an exact zoom percentage.

Use Page Break Preview

1. Choose **View, Page Break Preview**.

2. Click and drag the page break lines to adjust where your page breaks are set in your print area.

3. Choose **View, Normal** to return to the Normal view.

View Full Screen

1. Choose **View, Full Screen** to view the worksheet with only the Full Screen toolbar to close the full screen. You can move the mouse pointer to the top of the screen and the menu commands appear.

See Also Worksheet Map, Views

V
W
X

PART 4

POWERPOINT QUICK
REFERENCE

A
B
C

ACTION BUTTONS

Action buttons are special elements you can add to your
PowerPoint presentations to provide information or draw
attention to your presentation.

Add Action Buttons

1. Choose **Slide Show, Action Buttons**, and select the
   action option from the submenu.

2. Click and hold the mouse button in the location where
   you want the action button. Drag to the appropriate
   size and then release the mouse button to open the
   Action Setting dialog box.

Action when you click
the action button.

Action when you move the
mouse over the action button.

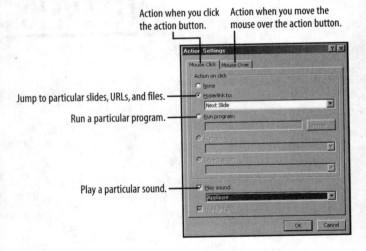

Jump to particular slides, URLs, and files.

Run a particular program.

Play a particular sound.

3. Select the action settings options and click the
   OK button to accept changes and return to the
   presentation.

4. Click the **Slide Show** button to see what the effect
   will look like. Click the actual **Action Button** to see
   how the action works. Press the Esc button on the keyboard to return to the Slide view.

See Also Slide Shows, Slide Transitions

ALIGNMENT

When you enter text into a presentation, the text automatically aligns flush (even) with the left margin. However, you can change the alignment of text at any time, before or after you have entered the text.

Quick Tips		
Feature	*Button*	*Keyboard Shortcut*
Align Left		Ctrl + L
Center		Ctrl + E
Align Right		Ctrl + R

Align Text

1. Select the text you want to align.
2. Choose **Format**, **Alignment**, and select the alignment type from the submenu.

See Also Format Text, Page Setup, Text

ANIMATION EFFECTS

PowerPoint's animation effects can bring presentations to life, making it hard for people to ignore information. You can apply animation to draw attention to especially relevant information.

Add Animation Effects

1. Select the object or text to which you want to add animation.
2. Click the **Animation Effects** button on the Formatting toolbar to open the Animation Effects toolbar. Click the effect you want to apply to the object.

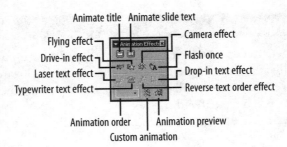

Animate title   Animate slide text

Flying effect — ┌ Camera effect
Drive-in effect — ┌ Flash once
Laser text effect — ┌ Drop-in text effect
Typewriter text effect — └ Reverse text order effect

Animation order   Animation preview
            Custom animation

3. Click the **Close** ☒ button to close the Animation Effects toolbar, or choose **View, Toolbars, Animation Effects** to toggle the toolbar closed.

See Also Action Buttons, Slide Shows, Slide Transitions

AUTOCONTENT WIZARD

PowerPoint helps you organize the ideas in your presentation through its AutoContent Wizard, which creates your presentation quickly, including a title slide and several slides to help you come up with information.

Start an AutoContent Wizard Presentation

1. Start PowerPoint, click the **AutoContent Wizard** option in the PowerPoint opening dialog box, and click the [OK] button. Or, if you are already in PowerPoint, choose **File, New; General** tab, and then double-click **AutoContent Wizard**.

2. Read the Welcome information in the AutoContent Wizard dialog box, then choose [Next >].

3. Click the kind of presentation you want to create, then choose [Next >].

4. Click the output option you want to use, then choose [Next >].

5. Type the title of the presentation and any items you want included on each slide, then choose [Next >].

6. Click the [Finish] button to view the presentation PowerPoint creates.

See Also Design Templates, New Presentations

AUTOLAYOUTS

see Slides   pg 249

BACKGROUNDS

You can change the color, shade, pattern, or texture of your slide background, or even use a picture as a slide background.

Apply a Background Color

1. Choose **Format, Background** to open the Background dialog box.

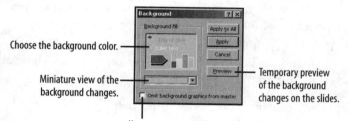

Choose the background color.

Miniature view of the background changes.

Temporary preview of the background changes on the slides.

Keeps any master slide graphics off the background display.

2. Select the background options and click to [Apply] the background to the current slide or [Apply to All] slides in the presentation.

Apply a Background Fill Effect

1. Choose **Format, Background** to open the Background dialog box. Click the **Color** drop-down list and select **Fill Effects** to open the Fill Effects dialog box.

2. Choose between the **Gradient, Texture, Pattern**, and **Picture** tabs to apply different effects. The **Sample** window in the bottom-right of the dialog box shows you what your background will look like. Click the [OK] button to accept changes and return to the Background dialog box.

3. Click the appropriate button to [Apply] the background to the current slide, [Apply to All] slides in the presentation, or click the [Cancel] button to not apply the changes.

See Also Colors and Lines

BLANK PRESENTATION

see Presentations   pg 246

COLORS AND LINES

You can add colors and lines to any or all sides of a text box or an object. This can make your presentation stand out and add variety to text-based slides.

Add Text Box Colors and Lines

1. Select the text box you want to alter.

2. Choose **Format, Colors and Lines** to open the **Colors and Lines** tab of the Format AutoShape dialog box.

3. Select the **Fill (Color)** and **Line (Color** and **Dashed)** options and click the ⬚ OK ⬚ button to accept changes and return to the presentation.

See Also Drawing Tools, Fonts, Lists, Text

CLIP ART

Clip art adds visual interest to your PowerPoint presentations. You can choose from numerous professionally prepared images.

Insert Clip Art

1. Click the **Clip Art** 🖼 button on the Drawing toolbar to open the Insert ClipArt dialog box.

2. Click the **Categories** of clip art in the **Pictures** tab and scroll through the options. To view more pictures, click **Keep Looking** at the bottom of the group of pictures.

3. Click the piece of clip art and choose **Insert Clip** 🖼 from the pop-up menu, which inserts the clip art into your presentation. Click the **Close** ✖ button to close the Insert ClipArt dialog box.

See Also Drawing Tools

CLIPBOARD

see Copy and Cut   pgs 235-236

CLOSE PRESENTATIONS

When you finish working on a presentation, you can close it and continue to work on other presentations. You can close a file with or without saving changes.

Quick Tips		
Feature	*Button*	*Keyboard Shortcut*
Close Presentation	☒ 🗐	Ctrl + F4 or Ctrl + W

Close a Presentation

1. Click the **Close** ☒ button. If you changed the presentation, PowerPoint asks you whether you want to save it.
2. Click the [Yes] button to save changes and close the presentation. Click the [No] button to close the presentation without saving changes, or click the [Cancel] button to return to working in your presentation without closing it or saving any changes.

See Also Save Presentations

COPY AND CUT

You can share information within slides and between presentations in PowerPoint by copying and cutting text and objects. You can now copy and cut up to 12 different items onto the Clipboard at a time. The Clipboard is where items are stored before you paste them.

Quick Tips		
Feature	*Button*	*Keyboard Shortcut*
Copy	🖺	Ctrl + C or Ctrl + Insert
Copy Format		Ctrl + ◆Shift + C
Copy Text Only		◆Shift + F2
Cut	✂	Ctrl + X or ◆Shift + Del

Copy

1. Select the text or object you want to copy.

2. Click the **Copy** button on the Standard toolbar. The original text remains in this location and a copy is placed on the Clipboard ready to be pasted.

Cut

1. Select the text or object you want to cut.

2. Click the **Cut** button on the Standard toolbar. This removes the text from the location and places it on the Clipboard ready to be pasted.

Copy Multiple Items

1. Choose **View, Toolbars, Clipboard** to open the Clipboard toolbar.

2. Select an item you want to copy and click the **Copy** button on the Clipboard toolbar after each time you select an item (up to 12 items). You can also use the **Copy** and **Cut** buttons on the Standard toolbar to place items on the Clipboard toolbar.

Paste all items in the presentation.   Delete all items from the Clipboard.

Copy an item to the Clipboard.   Paste an item into the presentation.

3. Move the mouse pointer over the Clipboard items and a ScreenTip displays what is contained in each copied clip (unless the clip is extensive, then only part of it displays). Click the clip to paste the item in the presentation. Click the **Close** button to close the Clipboard toolbar.

> **TIP**
>
> The Clipboard toolbar automatically appears when you click either the **Cut** 📈 or **Copy** 📋 buttons multiple times. Click the **Close** ☒ button to close the Clipboard toolbar, or choose **View, Toolbars, Clipboard** to toggle the toolbar closed.

See Also Format Painter, Move Text, Objects, Paste

DELETE SLIDES
see Slides pg 249

DESIGN TEMPLATES

Design templates are preset schemes that maintain a consistent look between colorful graphics, backgrounds, bullets, and fonts. You can change the design template as many times as you want when working in a presentation.

Start a Design Template Presentation

1. Start PowerPoint, click the **Design Template** option in the PowerPoint opening dialog box, and click the [OK] button. Or, if you are already in PowerPoint choose **File, New; Design Templates** tab and double-click the design template.

2. Click a design template and the **Preview** area gives you an idea of what it will look like. Click the [OK] button.

3. Click the type of slide you want to begin with in the **Choose an AutoLayout** area, and click the [OK] button.

Apply Design Templates

1. Click the [Common Tasks ▾] button on the Formatting toolbar and choose **Apply Design Template** from the submenu.

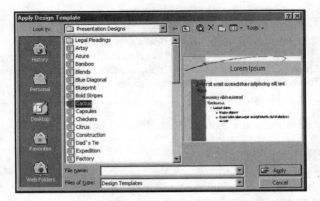

2. Select the design template from the Presentation Designs folder; a preview appears on the right side of the Apply Design Template dialog box.

3. Click the **Apply** button and the design template background and colors are applied to all slides in the presentation.

See Also Backgrounds, Slide Color Scheme, Slide Layout, Slide Master

DRAWING TOOLS

PowerPoint provides many tools for you to draw and format shapes and text boxes in your presentation.

Draw Shapes

1. Click the shape you want to draw in your presentation: **Line** ◲, **Arrow** ◳, **Rectangle** ◱, **Oval** ◴.

2. Click in the presentation and drag the crosshatch pointer to the desired shape size.

Add Shape Color

1. Click the shape you want to color in your presentation.

2. Click the appropriate button to select how you want to apply the color: **Fill Color** ◩ and **Line Color** ◪. Click the desired color.

Alter Shape Style

1. Click the shape you want to style in your presentation.

2. Click the appropriate button to select how you want to apply the style: **Line Style** ▤, **Dash Style** ▦, **Arrow Style** ▤, **Shadow** ▢, **3-D** ◪. Choose the desired style.

Insert AutoShapes

1. Click the AutoShapes ▾ button on the Drawing toolbar and select the particular shape you want to add to your presentation from the submenus.

2. Click in the presentation and drag the crosshatch pointer to the desired shape size.

Rotate Shapes

1. Click the shape you want to rotate in your presentation.

2. Click the **Free Rotate** ⟳ button on the Drawing toolbar.

3. Click the rotate pointer on the object rotate handles and drag the object to the desired rotation.

Add a Text Box

1. Click the **Text Box** ▤ button on the Drawing toolbar, or choose **Insert**, **Textbox**.

2. Click in the presentation and drag the crosshatch pointer to the desired shape size.

3. Click the **Font Color** ▲ button and select the color for the font and type the information you want in the text box.

Add WordArt

1. Click the **WordArt** ◢ button on the Drawing toolbar.

2. Double-click a WordArt style in the WordArt Gallery dialog box and type the text in the Edit WordArt Text dialog box. Click the ▭ ok ▭ button to accept changes and return to the presentation.

See Also Clip Art, Colors and Lines, Objects, Text

EMAIL

You can send the contents of the current PowerPoint presentation as the substance of the email message or as an attachment. Refer to the **Outlook** section for more information on email.

Send Presentation As an Email

1. Click the **Mail Recipient** 🖻 button on the Standard toolbar and if prompted, choose the option to **Send the Current Slide As the Message Body** and click the ⬚ OK ⬚ button to continue.

2. Type the **To, Cc,** and any changes to the **Subject** line (should be the filename) and any other changes in the message. Click the ⬚ Send this Slide ⬚ button and it will be sent.

> **TIP**
>
> Click the **Mail Recipient** 🖻 button again if you decide not to send the email and want to return to the presentation.

Send Presentation As an Email Attachment

1. Choose **File, Send To, Mail Recipient (as Attachment)**. This opens an email message and inserts the current presentation as an attachment.

2. Type the **To, Cc,** and any changes to the **Subject** line (should be the filename) and any other changes in the document. Click the ⬚ Send ⬚ button and it will be sent.

See Also Web Pages

FIND TEXT

You can use PowerPoint's Find feature to locate text, characters, paragraph formatting, and special characters.

Quick Tips		
Feature	*Button*	*Keyboard Shortcut*
Find	🔍	Ctrl+F or ⬆Shift+F4
Browse Next		Ctrl+PgDn
Browse Previous		Ctrl+PgUp
Repeat Find		⬆Shift+F4 or Ctrl+Alt+Y

Find Regular Text

1. Choose **Edit**, **Find** to open the Find dialog box.

2. Type the text you want to locate into the **Find What** text box.

3. Click the button to move to each occurrence within the presentation. If there aren't any to be found, PowerPoint notifies you that it has finished searching the presentation and that the item wasn't found.

See Also Replace Text

FONTS

To draw attention to important words and phrases in a presentation, you can change the text font options.

D
E
F

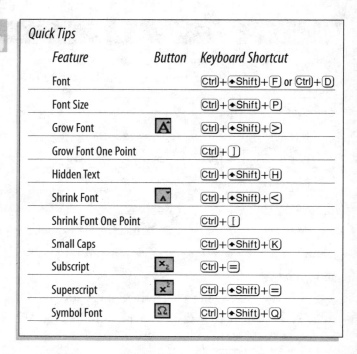

Quick Tips

Feature	Button	Keyboard Shortcut
Font		Ctrl+Shift+F or Ctrl+D
Font Size		Ctrl+Shift+P
Grow Font	A	Ctrl+Shift+>
Grow Font One Point		Ctrl+]
Hidden Text		Ctrl+Shift+H
Shrink Font	A	Ctrl+Shift+<
Shrink Font One Point		Ctrl+[
Small Caps		Ctrl+Shift+K
Subscript	x₂	Ctrl+=
Superscript	x²	Ctrl+Shift+=
Symbol Font	Ω	Ctrl+Shift+Q

Change Existing Font

1. Select the text in which you want to change the font.
2. Choose **Format, Font** to open the Font dialog box.

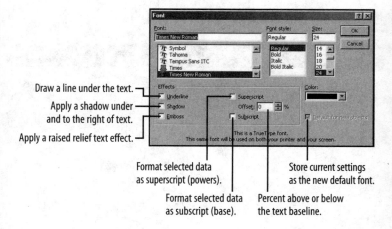

Draw a line under the text.

Apply a shadow under and to the right of text.

Apply a raised relief text effect.

Format selected data as superscript (powers).

Format selected data as subscript (base).

Percent above or below the text baseline.

Store current settings as the new default font.

3. Choose the **Font, Font Style, Size, Effects,** and **Color.** Click the [OK] button to accept changes and return to the presentation.

TIP

You can also select the font before you begin typing and it will become the current font when inserting new text objects.

See Also Drawing Tools, Text

FORMAT PAINTER

You can use the Format Painter to copy the format from a selected object or text and apply it to different objects or text you select.

Copy Character and Paragraph Formats

1. Select the text or object containing the format you want to copy and paste.
2. Click the **Format Painter** 🖌 button on the Standard toolbar.
3. Select the text or object where you want to apply the formatting; it formats automatically.

Copy Formats to Multiple Locations

1. Select the text or object containing the format you want to copy and paste. Double-click the **Format Painter** 🖌 button on the Standard toolbar.
2. Select each particular text or object to automatically apply the formatting. Click the **Format Painter** 🖌 button again when finished applying the format to multiple places.

See Also Copy and Cut, Paste

HEADER AND FOOTER

Headers and footers are text blocks that print at the top or bottom of every page in a presentation—headers at the top, footers at the bottom.

Insert Header and Footer

1. Choose **View**, **Header and Footer** to open the Header and Footer dialog box.

2. Select the options to apply to your slides, notes, and handouts.

Add the date and time.
Update the date and time automatically.
Change the date and time format.
Fix the date and time permanently.
Display the slide number.
Display the entered footer text.
Header and footer not to appear on the title slide.

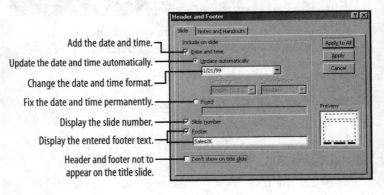

3. Click the appropriate button to [Apply] the background to the current slide, [Apply to All] slides in the presentation, or [Cancel] the changes.

TIP

To add a slide number to a single slide, select where you want the slide number to go on the presentation and choose **Insert**, **Slide Number**.

See Also Page Setup, Print Preview, Views

HYPERLINKS

When you click a hyperlink, the presentation appears to *jump* to the related location. You can type a hyperlink directly into your presentation or you can use the **Insert Hyperlink**  button on the Standard toolbar to manipulate the hyperlinks.

Quick Tips

Feature	Button	Keyboard Shortcut
Hyperlink		Ctrl + K

Type a URL Hyperlink Into a Presentation

1. Click the mouse pointer in the presentation where you want to add the hyperlink.

2. Type the URL into your presentation and the address automatically becomes a hyperlink. The text will be underlined in a different color.

3. Move the mouse pointer over the hyperlink and the location displays in a ScreenTip.

Insert a Hyperlink

1. Select the text that you want to make into a hyperlink.

2. Click the **Insert Hyperlink** button on the Standard toolbar to open the Insert Hyperlink dialog box.

3. Type the link into the **Type the File or Web Page Name** text box or select from the recent files, browsed pages, or inserted links list. Click the [OK] button to accept changes and return to the presentation.

Files recently worked on

Web pages recently browsed

Links recently used

TIP

To delete a hyperlink, right-click the hyperlink and choose **Hyperlink, Remove Hyperlink.** To edit a hyperlink, right-click the hyperlink and choose **Hyperlink, Edit Hyperlink.** Make the changes and click the [OK] button.

See Also Objects, Text, Save Presentations, Web Pages

LINE SPACING

Line spacing allows you to adjust the amount of vertical space between lines of text, before the first line of each selected paragraph, and after the last line of each selected paragraph.

Alter Line Spacing

1. Select the text for which you want to alter the line spacing.

2. Choose **Format, Line Spacing** to open the Line Spacing dialog box.

3. Click and select from the **Line Spacing, Before Paragraph**, and **After Paragraph** drop-down list options. Click the [OK] button to accept the changes and return to the presentation.

See Also Alignment, Page Setup

LISTS

You can select text and make it into a numbered or bulleted list. In addition, you can use a text box to begin typing a numbered or bulleted list.

Insert a List

1. Click the **Text Box** 🔲 button on the Drawing toolbar; click and drag the desired text box size in the presentation.
2. Click the **Numbering** 📑 button to begin a numbered list; click the **Bullets** 📑 button to begin a bulleted list.

Create a List

1. Select the lines of text you would like to make into a list.
2. Click the **Numbering** 📑 button to make it a numbered list; click the **Bullets** 📑 button to make it a bulleted list. Notice that a bullet is added to each paragraph, not each sentence.
3. Right-click the bullets and choose **Bullets and Numbering** from the shortcut menu.
4. Click the **Bulleted** or **Numbered** tab to choose the types of styles. Click the ▭ OK ▭ button to accept changes and return to the presentation.

See Also Drawing Tools

MASTERS

This is where you can set the default layout and formatting for all the slides in your presentation and for a title slide. This is similar to creating your own design template.

Create a Slide Master and Title Master

1. Choose **View, Master, Slide Master** to open the Slide Master view. Choose **View, Toolbars, Master** to open the Master toolbar, if it isn't already open.
2. Click to format the **Title Area, Object Area, Footer Area**, and **Number Area**. You can format the master slide with any colors, lines, and objects as well as add any action buttons, transitions, or features that you want each slide in your presentation to have.

3. Choose **Insert, New Title Master** to open a new title master. Click to edit the **Title Area**, **Subtitle Area**, **Date Area**, **Footer Area**, and **Number Area**. You can format the title master slide with any colors, lines, and backgrounds, as well as add any features that you want the initial title slide in your presentation to have.

4. Click the [Close] button on the Master toolbar to return to the original presentation view. Now any new slide you add to your presentation will contain the design template that you applied to the master slide. In addition, you can make edits to both masters at any time and the changes will apply to all slides in the presentation.

View the Slide Miniature

1. Choose **View, Master, Slide Master** to open the Slide Master view.

2. Choose **View, Toolbars, Master** to open the Master toolbar, if it isn't already open. Click the **Slide Miniature** 🖼 button to open the Slide Miniature window. Click the **Slide Miniature** 🖼 button again to close the window.

TIP

You can also create a **Handout Master** and **Notes Master**. Select either option from the **View, Master** submenu and format the master as you like.

See Also Design Templates, Views

MOVE TEXT

You can reorganize text in a PowerPoint presentation by moving items as you work. This method can be faster than cutting and pasting text.

Quick Tips	
Feature	*Keyboard Shortcut*
Move Text	F2

Move Text to a New Location

1. Click once to select the text box object you want to move.

2. Click the object again, drag the text box to the new location, and drop the text box in the new location.

See Also Copy and Cut, Objects, Paste

NEW PRESENTATIONS

You can use PowerPoint to plan every aspect of a winning presentation. PowerPoint even helps you organize the ideas in your presentation through its AutoContent Wizard, which quickly creates your presentation, including a title slide and several slides to help you come up with information.

Quick Tips		
Feature	*Button*	*Keyboard Shortcut*
New Presentation	🗋	Ctrl+N
New Slide	🖺	Ctrl+M

Start a New Blank Presentation

1. Start PowerPoint, click the **Blank Presentation** option in the PowerPoint opening dialog box, and click the [ok] button. Or, if you are already in PowerPoint, choose **File, New; General** tab and double-click **Blank Presentation**.

2. Click the **Blank** slide in the **Choose an AutoLayout** selection area and click the [ok] button.

Create a New Presentation

1. Click the **New** 🗋 button on the Standard toolbar and PowerPoint opens the New Slide dialog box.

2. Click in the **Choose an AutoLayout** section and click the [ok] button to begin working in the new presentation.

See Also AutoContent Wizard, Design Templates

OBJECTS

A PowerPoint object can be any of numerous types of elements that you add to your presentation: file, art, chart, worksheet, photo, movie, text clip, and so on.

Insert a New Object

1. Choose **Insert, Object; Create New** option.

2. Click the **Object Type** from the list box. Click the [OK] button to accept the changes and return to the presentation.

3. Click directly on the object and make any changes to it using the associated toolbar.

Insert an Object File

1. Choose **Insert, Object; Create from File** option. The Create new option allows you to create a new object file before you insert and link to it.

2. Type in the **File Name** or click the [Browse...] button to select the file from a specific location.

3. Select the **Link** option if you want the object to be linked to this presentation and the source file. This means that any changes you make in the source file will be reflected in your presentation. Click the [OK] button to accept changes and return to the presentation.

Resize Objects

1. Click once directly on a presentation and the object handles appear on all sides and corners of the object.

2. Move the mouse pointer over one of the handles, click and hold the handle once the pointer becomes a two-headed arrow.

3. Drag the handle to the desired size. If you drag from the corner handles, the height and width increases or decreases proportionately. If you drag from the side handles, only the height or width increases or decreases. Click elsewhere in the presentation to deselect the object.

Move Objects

1. Click once directly on a presentation and the object handles appear on all sides and corners of the object.
2. Move the mouse pointer over the object, click and hold the pointer when the pointer appears with a gray box below it. Drag the object to the new location and drop the object.

Delete Objects

1. Click once directly on a presentation and the object handles appear on all sides and corners of the object.
2. Press the Del key and the object is removed from the presentation.

TIP

If you link a worksheet object in your presentation, you can quickly edit or open the source file by double-clicking the object. You can also copy, cut, and paste an object to a different location.

See Also Clip Art, Drawing Tools

OPEN PRESENTATIONS

Each time you want to work with a presentation, you need to open it using the Open dialog box.

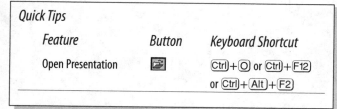

Quick Tips		
Feature	*Button*	*Keyboard Shortcut*
Open Presentation	🖼	Ctrl+O or Ctrl+F12 or Ctrl+Alt+F2

Open a Presentation

1. Click the **Open** 🖼 button on the Standard toolbar to display the Open dialog box listing the saved PowerPoint presentations.
2. Click the **Places Bar** option for the location of the file you want to open.

3. Click the **Look In** drop-down list to help locate the correct file or drive. You can also click the **Up One Folder** 🖼 button to move through folders.

4. Double-click the file you want to open and PowerPoint opens the presentation.

Open Files of Different Type

1. Click the **Open** 🖼 button on the Standard toolbar to display the Open dialog box listing the saved PowerPoint presentations.

2. Click the **Files of Type** drop-down list and select the file type. The Open dialog box displays only files that are of the type you selected.

3. Double-click the file you want to open and PowerPoint opens the presentation. If the file cannot be opened because there is a type mismatch, PowerPoint alerts you of this with a message box.

TIP

If you just started PowerPoint, you can click the **Open An Existing Presentation** option on the initial PowerPoint dialog box.

M N O

See Also New Presentations, Sample Presentations

OUTLINES

Quick Tips

Feature	Button	Keyboard Shortcut
Collapse	⊟	Alt + ⬆Shift + − or Alt + ⬆Shift + Num Lock −
Collapse All	≣	Alt + ⬆Shift + 1
Demote	⇨	Alt + ⬆Shift + →
Expand	⊞	Alt + ⬆Shift + = or Alt + ⬆Shift + Num Lock +
Expand All	≣	Alt + ⬆Shift + 9
Move Down	⬇	Alt + ⬆Shift + ↓
Move Up	⬆	Alt + ⬆Shift + ↑
Promote	⇦	Alt + ⬆Shift + ←
Show First Line		Alt + ⬆Shift + L
Summary Slide	▦	
Show Formatting	ᴬ⁄	

The Outline view enables you to work with headings and text on your slides. You can quickly move text to other slides and organize your information as a whole presentation review.

Work in Outline View

1. Click the **Outline View** button and choose **View, Toolbars, Outlining**, which displays the Outline toolbar in the Outline view.
2. Click the buttons on the Outline toolbar (refer to the Quick Tips section) to format headings and text throughout your presentation.

See Also Views, Workspace

PAGE SETUP

You can adjust the orientation and slide size for presentations.

Change the Page Setup

1. Choose **File, Page Setup** to open the Page Setup dialog box.

2. Select the **Slides Sized For** drop-down list (which automatically alters the **Width** and **Height** boxes—or you can click their spin boxes to change them).

3. Select the **Orientation** of **Portrait** or **Landscape** for either your **Slides** or **Notes, Handouts & Outline**. Click the [OK] button to accept changes and return to the presentation.

See Also Print

PASTE

You can share information within and between presentations in PowerPoint by pasting text and objects. You can now paste up to 12 different items from the Clipboard at a time. The Clipboard is where items are stored after you copy or cut them.

Quick Tips		
Feature	*Button*	*Keyboard Shortcut*
Paste	📋	Ctrl+V or ⇧Shift+Insert
Paste Format		Ctrl+⇧Shift+V

Paste Text or Objects

1. Place the cursor in the location where you want to place the text or object. You must have already cut or copied text or an object in order for the **Paste** 📋 button to be active.

2. Click the **Paste** 📋 button on the Standard toolbar.

Paste Multiple Items

1. Choose **View, Toolbars, Clipboard** to open the Clipboard toolbar. You must have already cut or copied text or an object for there to be any items on the Clipboard.

2. Place the cursor in the location where you want to insert a clip item.

Paste all items in the presentation.   Delete all items from the Clipboard.

Copy an item to the Clipboard.   Paste an item into the presentation.

3. Move the mouse pointer over the Clipboard items and a ScreenTip displays what is contained in each clip (unless the clip is extensive, then only part of it will display).

4. Click the clip that you want to paste. When finished, click the **Close** ☒ button to close the Clipboard toolbar, or choose **View, Toolbars, Clipboard** to toggle the toolbar closed.

Paste Special

1. Place the cursor in the location where you want to paste the text or object. You must have already cut or copied text or an object.

2. Choose **Edit, Paste Special** to open the Paste Special dialog box.

3. Select the **Paste** option to simply paste the item; select **Paste Link** to create a shortcut link to the source file (any changes you make to the source file are reflected automatically in your presentation). The **Paste Link** option won't be available if your copied selection isn't linkable.

4. Select the **As** option for how you want to paste the item. The **Result** area of the dialog box explains each type of paste. Click the ▭ OK ▭ button to accept changes and return to the presentation.

See Also Copy and Cut, Hyperlink, Move Text, Replace Text

PRINT

In PowerPoint you can print different versions of your presentation as you need them.

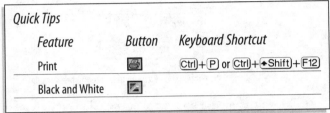

Quick Tips

Feature	Button	Keyboard Shortcut
Print		Ctrl+P or Ctrl+⬆Shift+F12
Black and White		

Print Current Presentation Defaults

Click the **Print** button on the Standard toolbar; the presentation prints according to the settings in your page setup.

Print a Presentation

1. Choose **File**, **Print** to open the Print dialog box.

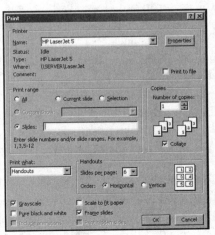

2. Select the **Print Range** options and number of **Copies** for the presentation.

3. Click the **Print What** drop-down arrow and choose to print just the **Slides, Handouts** for your audience, **Notes Pages,** or the **Outline View**. If you choose to print **Handouts,** click the number of **Slides Per Page** you want.

4. Click the ▭ OK ▭ button and the presentation prints.

Choose a Different Printer

1. Choose **File, Print** to open the Print dialog box.

2. Click the **Name** drop-down list and select to which printer you want to print. Click the ▭ OK ▭ button and the presentation prints.

See Also Page Setup

REDO
see Undo   pg 252

REHEARSE TIMINGS
see Slide Shows   pg 249

REPLACE TEXT

In PowerPoint, you can replace text, data formats, and special characters.

Quick Tips	
Feature	*Keyboard Shortcut*
Replace	Ctrl + H

Search and Replace Text

1. Choose **Edit, Replace** to open the Find and Replace dialog box.

2. Type the text you want to locate in the **Find What** text box. Any text from a previous search will still be in the dialog box, unless you have exited PowerPoint.

3. Click in the **Replace With** text box (or press the `Tab⇆` key) and type the text you want to replace it with.

4. Select from the search options and click the appropriate action button.

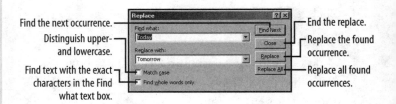

Find the next occurrence. — End the replace.

Distinguish upper- and lowercase. — Replace the found occurrence.

Find text with the exact characters in the Find what text box. — Replace all found occurrences.

See Also Copy and Cut, Find Data, Move Data, Paste, Redo and Undo

SAMPLE PRESENTATIONS

PowerPoint comes with several presentation templates that were created for various types of presentations and situations. These templates have basic artistic features and usually a skeleton outline you can fill in or expand on.

Use a Sample Presentation

1. Choose **File**, **New**; **Presentations** tab.

2. Click a presentation template. The preview area shows an example of what it will look like. Click the [OK] button. PowerPoint opens the generic presentation template.

See Also Design Templates, New Presentations, Open Presentations

SAVE PRESENTATIONS

Save the presentation you are working in to store it for later retrieval. A good practice is to save your presentations frequently as you work in them.

Quick Tips

Feature	Button	Keyboard Shortcut
Save	🖫	Ctrl + S or ⬆Shift + F12
		or Alt + ⬆Shift + F2
Save As		F12

Save a Presentation

1. Click the **Save** 🖫 button on the Standard toolbar to save any recent changes. If you haven't saved the presentation yet, the Save As dialog box appears.

2. Click the **Places Bar** option for the location of the file you want to save. Click the **Save In** drop-down list to help locate the correct folder or drive. You can also click the **Up One Folder** 🖻 button to move through folders.

3. Type the **File Name** and click the 🖫 Save button.

Save As a Different Name

1. Choose **File, Save As** to open the Save As dialog box.

2. Click the **Places Bar** option for the location of the file you want to save. Click the **Save In** drop-down list to help locate the correct folder or drive. You can also click the **Up One Folder** 🖻 button to move through folders.

3. Type the new **File Name** and click the 🖫 Save button.

Save As a Different File Type

1. Choose **File, Save As** to open the Save As dialog box.

2. Click the **Places Bar** option for the location of the file you want to save. Click the **Save In** drop-down list to help locate the correct folder or drive. You can also click the **Up One Folder** 🖻 button to move through folders.

3. Click the **Save as Type** drop-down list and select the desired file type. Type the **File Name** and click the 🖫 Save button.

See Also Close Presentations, Open Presentations, Web Pages

S
T
U

SEARCH
see Replace Text   pg 247

SLIDES

Slides in a presentation are similar to pages in a document and worksheets in a workbook. You can add, delete, copy, and even create them from other files and presentations.

Quick Tips		
Feature	*Button*	*Keyboard Shortcut*
New Slide	🔲	Ctrl+M
Duplicate Slide		Ctrl+⬆Shift+D or Ctrl+D

Add and Delete Slides

1. Click the **New Slide** 🔲 button on the Standard toolbar to add a new slide.

2. Double-click the kind of slide you want in the New Slide dialog box. Notice that PowerPoint adds the new slide to the Outline pane.

3. Click a slide or on a slide number in the Outline pane. Choose **Edit, Delete Slide** to delete the slide.

Duplicate Slides

1. Click the slide you want to duplicate in the Outline pane.

2. Choose **Edit, Duplicate** to duplicate the slide outline.

Create Slides from Files

1. Choose **Insert, Slides from Files; Find Presentation** tab to open the Slide Finder dialog box. Click the Browse... button to locate the presentation you want to insert a slide from.

2. Double-click the presentation and select the slides and options you want to insert.

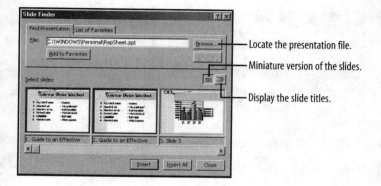

- Locate the presentation file.
- Miniature version of the slides.
- Display the slide titles.

3. Click the appropriate button to [Insert] the slide, [Insert All] slides, or to [Close] the dialog box and return to the presentation.

Create Slides from Outlines

1. Choose **Insert, Slides from Outlines** to open the Insert Outline dialog box.

2. Double-click the file that contains an outline with heading levels and normal body text. PowerPoint converts the outline to slides.

See Also Slide Master, Design Templates

SLIDE COLOR SCHEME

You can reapply or modify your existing color scheme or make changes to another color scheme you want to apply.

Alter the Color Scheme

1. Choose **Format, Slide Color Scheme** to open the Color Scheme dialog box.

Create custom scheme colors.

View new color settings in the presentation temporarily.

Delete a scheme color.

2. Select the color scheme you want to apply. Click to
   Apply the color scheme to the current slide, Apply to All
   slides in the presentation, or Cancel the changes.

See Also Background, Design Templates

SLIDE DESIGN

Although you can alter the individual look of your slides,
PowerPoint provides numerous design templates you can
immediately apply to your presentation.

Change the Slide Design

1. Click the Common Tasks ▾ button on the Formatting toolbar
   and choose **Apply Design Template** from the submenu.

2. Click the design you want to apply from the
   Presentation Designs list box.

3. Click the Apply button on the Apply Design dialog
   box.

See Also Design Templates, Slides, Slide Layout

SLIDE LAYOUT

PowerPoint's AutoLayouts are preset styles for the layout of your slides. You are asked to apply them when you create a new presentation, new slide, and can change them at any time.

Change the Slide Layout

1. Click the Common Tasks button on the Formatting toolbar and choose **Slide Layout** from the submenu. Or choose **Format**, **Slide Layout** to open the Slide Layout dialog box.

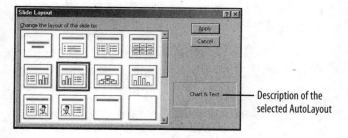

Description of the selected AutoLayout

2. Click the AutoLayout you want to reapply to your current slide and click the OK button. The layout style will be applied even if there is already information on your slide.

See Also Design Templates, New Presentation, Slides, Slide Design

SLIDE MASTER
see Masters   pg 244

SLIDE MINIATURE
see Masters   pg 244

SLIDE SHOW

When people begin creating presentations, they usually have a specific time limit they need to follow. Instead of using your watch and trying to time the show yourself, let PowerPoint do the work for you.

Quick Tips

Feature	Keyboard Shortcut
Next Slide	Ⓝ; ⏎Enter; Spacebar
Previous Slide	Ⓟ or ⬅Backspace
Go to Slide (*number*)	(*number*)+⏎Enter
Toggle Black Screen	Ⓑ
Toggle White Screen	Ⓦ
Stop Slide Show	Ⓢ
End Slide Show	Esc
Erase Onscreen Annotations	Ⓔ
Next Hidden Slide	Ⓗ
New Rehearsal Timings	Ⓣ
Use Original Rehearsal Timings	Ⓞ
Use Click to Advance Rehearsing	Ⓜ
Return to First Slide	Both Mouse buttons two seconds
Pointer to a Pen	Ctrl+Ⓟ
Pen to a Pointer	Ctrl+Ⓐ
Hide Pointer Temporary	Ctrl+Ⓗ
Hide Pointer Always	Ctrl+Ⓛ
Display Shortcut Menu	⬆Shift+F10
List of Controls	F1

View a Slide Show

1. Click the **Slide Show** 🖥 button on the View toolbar with your presentation open.

2. Press the ⎵Spacebar⎵ to display the next slide. You can press the ⎵Esc⎵ key to stop the slide show anywhere in the presentation.

Rehearse a Presentation

1. Choose **Slide Show**, **Rehearse Timings** to run through a rehearsal of your slide show. The Rehearsal toolbar automatically appears.

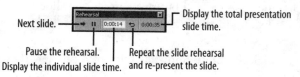

Next slide. ——— | Display the total presentation slide time.

Pause the rehearsal.
Display the individual slide time. | Repeat the slide rehearsal and re-present the slide.

2. Rehearse your slide show and move through each of the slides as you would perform them. The timings will stop at the end of the last slide in the presentation, or you can click the **Close** ☒ button to stop the rehearsal.

3. Click the ⎡ Yes ⎤ button when asked if you want to record your slide show times. These will be displayed in the Slide Sorter view. If you do not want to, click the ⎡ No ⎤ button to return to the presentation.

See Also Slide Sorter

SLIDE SORTER

The Slide Sorter view displays a small version of your slides. This enables you to rearrange your slides and view slide details like action buttons, transition effects, animation effects, and rehearsal timings.

Reorder Slides

1. Click the **Slide Sorter View** 🔡 button to view the slide sorter.

2. Click the slide and drag the mouse pointer to the desired location. Then release the mouse button to drop the slide in the new location.

See Also Slides, Views

SLIDE TRANSITIONS

Slide transitions are effects that introduce your slide in a slide show. These can make your presentations look more professional and interesting.

Add Slide Transitions

1. Choose **Slide Show, Slide Transition** to open the Slide Transition dialog box.

2. Click the **Effect** drop-down arrow and choose the transition you want to use.

3. Click the ⬚Apply to All⬚ button to apply the slide transition to all slides in the presentation or the ⬚Apply⬚ button to apply to the current slide.

4. Click the **Slide Show** ▣ button to preview the effect.

See Also Slides, Slide Shows, Slide Sorter View

SPELLING

You can check spelling in PowerPoint 2000 quickly and easily. Of course, you should always review your presentations, but it never hurts to have a little help.

Quick Tips		
Feature	*Button*	*Keyboard Shortcut*
Spelling	🔤	F7
Next Misspelling		Alt + F7

Check Spelling

1. Click the **Spelling and Grammar** 🔤 button on the Standard toolbar. The Spelling dialog box opens, displaying the first spelling error it finds.

2. Click the appropriate spelling option in the **Suggestions** list box; if one doesn't work, type the change directly in the **Change to** text box.

3. Click the appropriate button to make the selected **Suggestions** change.

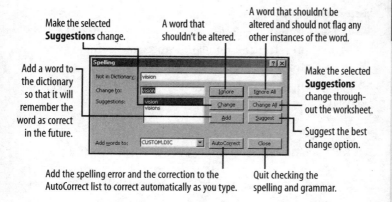

Make the selected **Suggestions** change.

A word that shouldn't be altered.

A word that shouldn't be altered and should not flag any other instances of the word.

Add a word to the dictionary so that it will remember the word as correct in the future.

Make the selected **Suggestions** change throughout the worksheet.

Suggest the best change option.

Add the spelling error and the correction to the AutoCorrect list to correct automatically as you type.

Quit checking the spelling and grammar.

4. Click the [OK] button if PowerPoint displays a message telling you the spelling check is complete. This means all inaccuracies have been reviewed.

See Also Text

TABLES

Instead of creating long lists of information and trying to cross-reference these lists, you can add a table to your presentation.

Draw Table

1. Click the **Tables and Borders Toolbar** [⊞] button on the Standard toolbar; the pointer becomes a pencil and the Tables and Borders toolbar opens.

2. Click in the presentation and drag to draw the outer border of the table. Click in the table and draw the rows and columns.

3. Click the **Draw Table** [✎] button on the Tables and Borders toolbar, which converts the pointer to a cursor so that you can add data to the table. Click the **Close** [✕] button to close the Tables and Borders toolbar, or choose **View, Toolbars, Tables and Borders** to toggle the toolbar closed.

Insert Table

1. Click the **Insert Table** ▦ button on the Standard toolbar and select the number of rows and columns you want from the drop-down box.

2. Click the cursor in the table cells and type to add the data.

Work with Columns

1. Move the mouse pointer over the right edge of the column you want to alter. When the mouse pointer changes to a two-headed arrow, click and drag the column to the new size.

2. Click the top border of a column (when the pointer becomes a black down arrow) to select it. Right-click and choose **Insert Columns** from the shortcut menu to add a column to the left of the selected column.

3. Right-click the column again and choose **Delete Columns** from the shortcut menu; that column will be deleted.

Work with Rows

1. Move the mouse pointer over the bottom edge of the row you want to alter. When the mouse pointer changes to a two-headed arrow, click and drag the row to the new size.

2. Click the left border of a row (when the pointer becomes a white right arrow) to select it. Right-click and choose **Insert Rows** from the shortcut menu to add a row above the selected row.

3. Right-click the row again and choose **Delete Rows** from the shortcut menu; that row will be deleted.

Format Tables and Borders

1. Select the table or cells that you want to format.

2. Choose **View, Toolbars, Tables and Borders** to open the Tables and Borders toolbar.

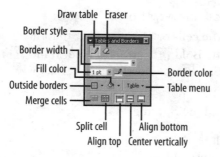

Draw table   Eraser
Border style
Border width
Fill color
Outside borders —————————————— Border color
Merge cells ————————————————— Table menu

Split cell   Align bottom
Align top   Center vertically

3. Click the desired formatting buttons and click the **Close** ☒ button to close the Tables and Borders toolbar, or choose **View**, **Toolbars**, **Tables and Borders** to toggle the toolbar closed.

TIP

To alter cell alignment, right-click a cell and choose **Cell Alignment** from the shortcut menu. Then, click the alignment style from the submenu.

See Also Apply Design Templates, Colors and Lines

TEXT

To draw attention to important text in a presentation, you can make the text any combination of bold, italic, underline, and shadow.

Quick Tips		
Feature	*Button*	*Keyboard Shortcut*
Bold	**B**	Ctrl + B
Italic	*I*	Ctrl + I
Underline	U	Ctrl + U
Shadow	S	

Format Bold, Italic, Underline, and Shadow

1. Select the cells or text you want to format.
2. Click the **Bold** ⯐ button to bold; **Italic** ⯐ to italicize; **Underline** ⯐ to underline; and **Shadow** ⯐ to shadow your text.

See Also Font, Line Spacing

TITLE MASTER
see Masters   pg 244

UNDO AND REDO

Undo and Redo are convenient when you want to see how your presentation looks with and without changes you make. In addition, this can be convenient when you have made an error in your worksheet.

Quick Tips		
Feature	*Button*	*Keyboard Shortcut*
Undo	⯐	Ctrl+Z or Alt+◄Backspace
Redo or Repeat	⯐	Ctrl+Y or Alt+↑Shift+◄Backspace or F4 or Alt+↵Enter

Use Undo and Redo

1. Type or make change(s) in your presentation.
2. Click the **Undo** ⯐ button as many times as necessary to undo the change(s).
3. Click the **Redo** ⯐ button as many times as necessary to redo the change(s).

> **TIP**
> You can also click the **Undo** or **Redo** drop-down list arrows to select the exact changes you want to make. In addition, this can be convenient when you have made an error in your worksheet.

See Also Close Presentations, Save Presentations

VIEWER

Perhaps someday you'll need to give a presentation using someone else's computer. If you're not sure PowerPoint is on their computer, you can create a Pack and Go presentation to view your presentation from anywhere.

Prepare the Presentation for Another Computer

1. Open the presentation you want to pack and choose **File, Pack and Go**. Read the welcome information on the **Pack and Go Wizard** dialog box, then choose `Next >`.

2. Click the **Active Presentation** option unless you want to choose to pack **Other Presentations(s)** and specify their file location, then choose `Next >`.

3. Click the **A:\ drive**, **B:\ drive**, or the **Choose Destination** option and specify the file location, then choose `Next >`.

4. Click **Include Linked Files** to deselect the default check box if you don't want to include linked files and click the **Embed TrueType Fonts** option if you want to keep your selected TrueType fonts, then choose `Next >`.

5. Click the **Viewer for Windows 95 or NT** option if you are going to give a presentation on a computer that doesn't have PowerPoint; otherwise keep the default **Don't Include the Viewer** option.

6. Click the `Next >` button and read the Finish information. Place a floppy disk in the particular drive (if that is the destination you chose), and click the `Finish` button. Click the `OK` button when a message appears, letting you know the presentation was packed successfully.

See Also Slide Shows

VIEWS

PowerPoint provides several different ways to view presentations while creating or modifying them. Each view provides a different perspective on a presentation. The Normal view is a new feature in PowerPoint 2000.

Outline Pane—edit the text throughout the presentation.

Slide Pane—edit the slides directly.

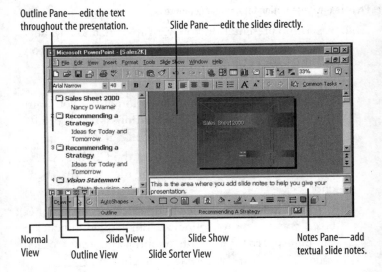

Normal View

Slide View

Slide Show

Notes Pane—add textual slide notes.

Outline View

Slide Sorter View

Work in Different Views

1. Click the **Outline View** ▣ button. You can add text, and both the Slide and Notes panes are still visible.

2. Click the **Slide View** ▢ button. You can add both text and art on a slide-by-slide basis and move through the presentation with the Outline pane.

3. Click the **Slide Sorter View** ▦ button. This enables you to rearrange your slides and view slide details like action buttons.

4. Click the **Slide Show** ▣ button. This enables you to view your slides as they would appear in a slide show. (Press the Esc key to return from the Slide Show view.)

See Also Slide Master, Slide Miniature, Slide Sorter

WEB PAGES

You can view your presentations as Web pages in Web Page Preview even before you have saved the file as a Web page.

Quick Tips

Feature	Keyboard Shortcut
Web Go Back	(Alt)+(←)
Web Go Forward	(Alt)+(→)

Use Web Page Preview

Choose **File, Web Page Preview** to open the Internet Explorer browser and display the presentation. Click the **Close** ☒ button to return to the PowerPoint presentation.

Save As a Web Page

1. Choose **File, Save As Web Page** to open the Save As dialog box.

2. Click the **Places Bar** option for the location of the file you want to save. Click the **Save In** drop-down list to help locate the correct folder. You can also click the **Up One Folder** 🔝 button to move through folders.

3. Click the ⌊Change Title...⌋ button and type in a **Page Title** if you want the page title to be different than the filename, and click the ⌊ ok ⌋ button. Note that you can click the ⌊Publish⌋ button to customize the Web page contents in one main Publish as a Web Page dialog box.

4. Type the **File Name** and click the ⌊🖫 Save⌋ button.

See Also Email, Save Presentations, Views

WORKSPACE

You can click the scrollbars to move the view of the presentation. Press the keys on the keyboard to move the cursor through the presentation, or view the rulers or full screen.

Quick Tips		
Feature	Button	Keyboard Shortcut
Word Left		Ctrl+←
Word Right		Ctrl+→
Minimize Presentation Window	▬	Ctrl+F9
Maximize Presentation Window	☐	Ctrl+F10
Move Presentation Window		Ctrl+F7
Restore Presentation Window	🗗	Ctrl+F5
Size Presentation Window		Ctrl+F8

Use Scrollbar Options

1. Click the Up and Down scrollbar arrows to scroll through the presentation. Click directly on the large scrollbar and drag it up and down to quickly move through the presentation.
2. Click the **Previous Slide** ⬆ and **Next Slide** ⬇ buttons to move through the presentation by slide.

View the Ruler and Guides

1. Choose **View, Ruler** to make the horizontal and vertical rulers display. Choose **View, Ruler** again to hide them.
2. Choose **View, Guides** to display the snap to guides in your slide. This helps with aligning objects. Choose **View, Guides** again to hide them.

Increase Presentation View Size

1. Click the **Zoom** drop-down list on the Standard toolbar.
2. Select the percentage or descriptive size you want to view your presentation in. You can also click directly on the **Zoom** list box and type in an exact zoom percentage.

See Also Views

Outlook Quick

Reference

**A
B
C**

ARCHIVE

You can periodically archive messages that are older than a particular date to an archive file that you specify.

Archive Messages

1. Choose **File**, **Archive** to open the Archive dialog box.

2. Select the option to **Archive All Folders According to Their AutoArchive Settings** or **Archive This Folder and All Subfolders**. If you choose the latter, click the folder you want to archive.

3. Click the **Archive Items Older Than** drop-down list box and select the appropriate date. Alter the Archive file location if you don't want it to be placed in the default folder. Click the [OK] button to perform the archive.

See Also AutoArchive, Folders

ATTACHMENTS

Many times you will send and receive email messages with file attachments. Attachments can be other emails, files, and graphics.

Attach Files

1. Click the **Attach** button on the Standard message toolbar when in an email message. Or, drag the file(s) and drop directly on the message portion of an email message.

2. Select the file(s) you want to attach and click the [Print] button; they will become icons in an attachments pane at the bottom of the email message.

View Attached Files

1. Click the **Attachments** ✐ button in the upper-right corner of the message Preview pane to see the attached file(s).

2. Click the filename and Outlook asks you if you want to open or save the file. If you click to open the file, it opens in the application it was created in (unless you don't have the application, then Outlook asks you what you want to try to open the file in). When you close the attached file, you return to Outlook.

Save Attached Files

1. Click a message with an attachment (ones with a paperclip in the header).

2. Choose **File, Save Attachments,** and select the file (or files) you want to save. If you select all the attachments, they must be saved in the same location; otherwise, select each attachment and save individually.

3. Click the 🖫 Save button to save the attachment with the same name the sender assigned it. Or, type a new filename and then click the 🖫 Save button.

See Also Receive Messages, Send Messages

AUTOARCHIVE

You can set AutoArchive to automatically move old items into an archive file and empty your Deleted Items folder.

Set AutoArchive Options

1. Choose **Tools, Options; Other** tab. Click the AutoArchive... button to set options for storing old items to an archive file.

2. Select the option to **Archive Every (*number of*) Days** and choose the number of days with the spin box control. Alter the **Default Archive File** location if you want it placed in a different folder and click the OK button. Click the OK button to accept changes.

See Also Archive, Delete Messages

CALENDAR

Using Outlook's Calendar view you can schedule appointments, meetings, and events.

A
B
C

Quick Tips		
Feature	*Button*	*Keyboard Shortcut*
Create Appointment	🔲	Ctrl + ↑Shift + A
Select Next Appointment		Tab↹
Select Previous Appointment		↑Shift + Tab↹
Delete Appointment	✕	Ctrl + D
Meeting Request		Ctrl + ↑Shift + Q
View 1 Day	1	Alt + 1
View 2 - 9 Days		Alt + (*number of days*)
View 10 Days		Alt + 0
Switch to Weeks	7	Alt + −
Switch to Months	31	Alt + = or
		Alt + ↑Shift + =

View Your Schedule

1. Click the **Calendar** shortcut on the Outlook Bar or click the **Calendar** option in Outlook Today.

View today's schedule.   View a 5-day work week.   View a month.

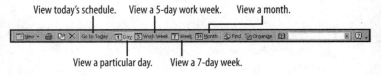

View a particular day.   View a 7-day week.

2. Click the buttons on the Calendar toolbar to view different date and time periods.

Schedule an Appointment

1. Select the appointment date, then click and drag the hours to schedule a time slot.

2. Type the description of the appointment and press the (↵Enter) key. Move the mouse pointer over the appointment on the calendar and the entire appointment information line appears in a ScreenTip.

Reschedule an Appointment

1. Select the appointment on the calendar.

2. Click and drag the appointment to the new date and time on the calendar.

Cancel an Appointment

1. Select the appointment on the calendar.

2. Click the **Delete** ⊠ button and the appointment disappears.

Schedule a Recurring Appointment

1. Select the appointment date, and then click and drag the hours to schedule a time slot.

2. Type the description of the appointment and press the (↵Enter) key. Double-click the appointment to open the Appointment window.

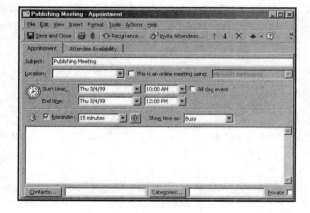

3. Click the ⟨🔄 Recurrence...⟩ button to open the Appointment Recurrence dialog box. If the selected appointment needs to have a different date and time, make the appropriate changes.

4. Click the ⟨ OK ⟩ button to return to the Appointment window and choose the ⟨💾 Save and Close⟩ button. Outlook adds a recurring appointment icon on the calendar at the appointment time.

Plan a Meeting

1. Select the time on your calendar that you would like to schedule a meeting. Choose **File, New, Meeting Request** to open the Meeting window. Click the **Attendee Availability** tab.

2. Type the name of the attendees in the **All Attendees** box. Press the ⟨↵Enter⟩ key and repeat this for each attendee. Or, click the ⟨Invite Others...⟩ button to select multiple individuals from the Select Attendees and Resources dialog box. If you are at a site that uses Exchange server for messaging, the attendee availability may display with color-coded descriptions.

3. Click the **Appointment** tab, then type the **Subject** of the meeting, **Location** where the meeting will be held, and any notes about the meeting in the lower text box.

4. Click the ⟨📧 Send ▾⟩ button on the Meeting toolbar and the meeting notification will be sent via email and listed on the Outlook calendar.

TIP

When others who use Outlook receive your meeting request, they can reply with **Accept, Tentative**, or **Decline**. This comes back to you as an email message noting their response. When they accept or tentatively accept, Outlook automatically puts the meeting on their calendar.

Schedule an Event

1. Right-click the day on your calendar and choose **New Recurring Event** from the shortcut menu to schedule an event like a birthday, quarterly meeting, or vacation days.

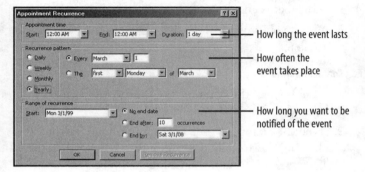

— How long the event lasts

— How often the event takes place

— How long you want to be notified of the event

2. Select the event information in the Appointment Recurrence dialog box and click the ☐ OK ☐ button.

3. Type the **Subject** of the event, **Location** where the event will be held, and any notes about the event in the lower text box.

4. Click the 🖫 Save and Close button. Outlook adds the event to your calendar.

See Also Contacts, Journal Entries, Preferences, Tasks

CONTACTS

You can create a contact list that contains business and personal contact information. The list is an electronic version of an address book or card file.

Quick Tips

Feature	Button	Keyboard Shortcut
Show Address Book		Ctrl + ⬆Shift + B
Create New Contact		Ctrl + ⬆Shift + C
Create Distribution List		Ctrl + ⬆Shift + L
Delete Contact		Ctrl + D

Create a Contact

1. Click the **Contacts** button on the Outlook Bar. Click the button on the Standard toolbar.

2. Type the contact information, pressing the `Tab⇆` key to move between text boxes.

3. When you finish, choose 🖫 Save and Close on the Contacts toolbar.

Edit Contact Information

1. Double-click the contact you want to edit, which will open the Contact window.

2. Type the changes to the contact information, then press the `Tab⇆` key to move between text boxes. Click the 🖫 Save and Close button on the Contacts toolbar.

TIP

To delete a contact, click the contact to select it and then click the **Delete** ☒ button on the Contacts toolbar.

See Also Calendar, Preferences, Tasks

DELETE MESSAGES

Just like regular mail, email has *junk* mail you will not want to keep in your Inbox. Or, perhaps you want to delete a message that is in your Outbox waiting to be sent.

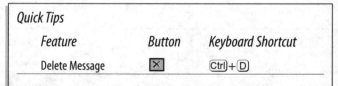

Quick Tips		
Feature	*Button*	*Keyboard Shortcut*
Delete Message	☒	`Ctrl`+`D`

Delete a Message

1. Click the message you want to delete. Click the **Delete** button on the Standard toolbar and the message is placed in the **Deleted Items** folder.

2. Right-click the Deleted Items folder and choose **Empty "Deleted Items" Folder** from the shortcut menu. Click the [Yes] button to permanently delete the message or click the [No] button if you decide you don't want to delete it yet.

> **TIP**
>
> If you decide you want to keep a deleted message, you can click the message in the Deleted Items folder and drag it into a different folder.

See Also Archive Messages, Folders

EXPORT MESSAGES

Perhaps you have numerous messages that you need to review but you don't have access to your email files; you can export the messages to a file and read them in a different application.

Export to a File

1. Choose **File, Import and Export** to open the Import and Export Wizard. Click the **Export to a File** option and click the [Next >] button.

2. Select the type of file you want to create and click the [Next >] button. Click the folder you want to export from and click the [Next >] button.

3. Type in a location and filename to save the exported file and click the [Next >] button. Review the action to be performed and click the [Finish] button.

> **TIP**
>
> Comma Separated Values (Windows) is a common file type to export messages as if you want to open them in Microsoft Word.

See Also Folders, Import Messages

F

212

FLAG MESSAGES

When you flag a message, you are creating a reminder that you need to follow up on the message.

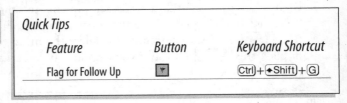

Quick Tips

Feature	Button	Keyboard Shortcut
Flag for Follow Up		Ctrl + ↑Shift + G

Flag a Message

1. Click the message you want to flag or click the message that is already flagged and choose **Actions, Flag for Follow Up** to open the Flag for Follow Up dialog box.

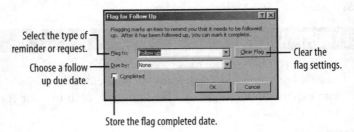

Select the type of reminder or request.

Choose a follow up due date.

Clear the flag settings.

Store the flag completed date.

2. Select the flagging mark options and click the [OK] button to accept changes. The closed message header contains a flag icon and the opened message header lists the type of flag and any due dates.

See Also Importance, Receive Messages, Send Messages

FOLDERS

The Inbox, Outbox, Sent Items, Drafts, and Deleted Items folders are the default Outlook folders. In addition, you can move, delete, and create folders.

Quick Tips		
Feature	*Button*	*Keyboard Shortcut*
Create New Folder	🖼	Ctrl + ⇧Shift + E
Go To Folder		Ctrl + Y
Delete Folder		Ctrl + D

Create a New Folder

1. Choose **File, New, Folder** to open the Create New Folder dialog box.

2. Type the **Name** of the folder, click the **Folder Contains** drop-down list to select the type of items, and click in the **Select Where To Place the Folder** list box. Click the ▭ ok ▭ button and the new folder is created. If Outlook asks you whether you want to create an Outlook Bar shortcut, click either the ▭ Yes ▭ or ▭ No ▭ buttons and possibly the **Don't Prompt Me About This Again** check box. A Folder List appears, so you can access the folder you created.

Move a Folder

1. Choose **View, Folder List** to open the Folder List pane, if it isn't already open. Or, click the **Folder List** 🖼 button to view the Folder List.

2. Click the folder you want to move, and then drag and drop it in the new Folder List location.

Delete a Folder

1. Select the folder you want to delete and click the **Delete** ✕ button on the Standard toolbar.

2. Outlook asks you whether you want to delete the folder and move all its contents into the Deleted Items folder. Click the ▭ Yes ▭ button to do so, or click the ▭ No ▭ button to cancel the delete.

See Also Workspace

FORWARD MESSAGES

Sometimes when you read a message, you find that the information would be pertinent to another individual. In that case, you can forward the message to that person.

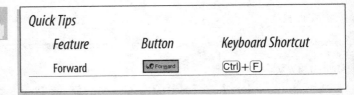

Quick Tips		
Feature	*Button*	*Keyboard Shortcut*
Forward	Forward	Ctrl+F

Forward a Message

1. Select the message you want to forward. Click the Forward button on the Standard toolbar to open the message in a new window.

2. Type the email address of the person to whom you want to forward the message and any other recipients. Type the rest of the message and click the Send button to send the message. Notice that the message contains a forward flag and the **Subject** line contains **RE:** to signify the message was forwarded.

See Also Receive Messages, Reply to Messages, Send Messages

IMPORTANCE

A message icon displays if an email has been marked for a specific level of importance.

Mark Message Importance

Click the **High** or **Low** buttons on the Standard message toolbar when writing a message. This lets the reader know that the message should be read immediately or can wait for later.

See Also Flag Messages

IMPORT MESSAGES

You can import message files from other applications into
Outlook to add them to your folders.

Import Message Files

1. Choose **File, Import and Export** to open the Import
   and Export Wizard. Click the **Import From Another
   Program of File** option and click the [Next >] button.

2. Select the type of file you want to import and click the
   [Next >] button. Type in a location and filename to
   import and select the option for how you want to handle duplicate messages, then click the [Next >] button.

3. Click the **Select Destination Folder** to save the
   imported messages and click the [Next >] button.
   Review the action to be performed and click the
   [Finish] button.

See Also Contacts, Export Messages

INBOX
see Receive Messages pg 247

JOURNAL ENTRIES

The Journal feature gives you one place in which to record
activities, such as talking to a contact, writing a mail message, or working on a file, as well as appointments, tasks,
and notes.

Quick Tips

Feature	Button	Keyboard Shortcut
Create Journal Entry	📧	Ctrl + Shift + J
Delete Journal Entry	✕	Ctrl + D

Create a Journal Entry

1. Click the **Journal** button on the Outlook Bar, then click the **New Journal Entry** button on the Standard toolbar.

2. Type a subject in the **Subject** text box. Click the **Entry Type** drop-down arrow to select the type of task and click the **Save and Close** button.

3. Click the **Plus** button for the **Entry Type** to review the journal entry assigned.

TIP

To delete a journal entry in Journal view, right-click the journal entry you want to delete and choose **Delete** on the shortcut menu.

See Also Calendar, Contacts, Preferences, Tasks

MAIL DELIVERY

You can control the automation of how often Outlook checks for mail and when your outbound messages are sent.

Set Mail Delivery Controls

1. Choose **Tools, Options; Mail Delivery** tab.

2. Select the **Mail Account Options** to control when Outlook automatically sends and receives messages. Choose to either **Send Messages Immediately When Connected** or **Check For New Messages Every (*number of*) Minutes**. If you choose the latter, click the spin box control to specify how often new messages are checked. Click the **OK** button to accept changes.

See Also Receive Messages, Send Messages

NEW MESSAGES

Creating email messages is perhaps the most common thing you'll do in Outlook.

Quick Tips

Feature	Button	Keyboard Shortcut
Create Message	🖼	Ctrl+⬆Shift+M

Create Email Messages

1. Click the 🔽New ▾ button on the Standard toolbar.
2. Type the recipient's email address in the **To** area and press the Tab⇥ key to move through and enter information into the **Cc**, **Subject**, and message areas.
3. Click the 🔽Send ▾ button to send your message.

> **TIP**
>
> Sometimes when writing an email you find that you aren't ready to send the message or you need to finish it at a different time. You can move these messages to the Drafts folder to complete and send later.

See Also Receive Messages, Send Messages

NOTES

You can use Outlook's Notes feature to jot down ideas, questions, reminders, directions, and anything you would write on paper. You can leave notes visible onscreen as you work.

Quick Tips

Feature	Button	Keyboard Shortcut
Create Note	📋	Ctrl+⬆Shift+N
Delete Note	☒	Ctrl+D

Create Notes

1. Click the **Notes** 📝 button on the Outlook Bar.
2. Click the **New Note** 📝 New ▾ button on the Standard toolbar. Type your note in the Note box.
3. Click in the Notes window to see the note. Any active notes also appear in your workspace.

TIP

To delete an open note, click the **Note** icon in the upper-left corner of the note and then choose **Delete** on the shortcut menu.

See Also Calendar, Journal Entries

OUTBOX
see Send Messages   pg 248

OUTLOOK TODAY

You can alter numerous options that are available in your Outlook Today view.

Alter Outlook Today Options

1. Click the **Customize Outlook Today** option while in the Outlook Today view.
2. Select from the **Startup, Messages, Calendar, Tasks,** and **Styles** options.
3. Click the **Save Changes** or **Cancel** options to return to Outlook Today with or without saving changes.

See Also Preferences, Workspace

PREFERENCES

You can customize the appearance of all the options in Outlook. Your changes will become the default settings as you work in Outlook.

Set Outlook Preferences

Choose **Tools, Options; Preferences** tab.

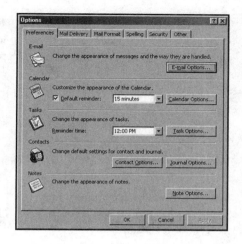

2. Select the Outlook preferences and click the OK button to accept the changes.

See Also Outlook Today, Workspace

PRINT

You can easily print as much or as little information from Outlook as you want. It can be convenient, however, to choose to preview before you print.

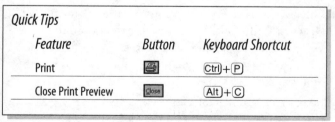

Quick Tips		
Feature	*Button*	*Keyboard Shortcut*
Print	🖨	Ctrl+P
Close Print Preview	Close	Alt+C

Print Preview

1. Choose **File, Print Preview** to see what your printout will look like.

2. Click the 🗐 Page Setup... button in Print Preview to alter the **Format, Paper,** and **Header/Footer** options. Click the OK button to accept your changes. Click the Cancel button to return to Outlook.

Print Mail Messages

1. Select the messages you want to print in a folder (press the ⟨⬆Shift⟩ key and click each message) or double-click a message to open the message window.

2. Click the **Print** 🖳 button on the Standard toolbar to print the message(s).

Print the Calendar

1. Click the **Print** 🖳 button on the Standard toolbar to open the Print dialog box.

2. Select the **Print Style** as to whether you want to print the **Daily, Weekly, Monthly, Tri-Fold,** or **Calendar Details** style of information.

3. Click the **Print Range** drop-down list boxes of **Start** and **End** to determine the dates of the calendar to print. You can also select whether you want private appointments printed.

4. Select the **Number of Copies** and click the ⟨ OK ⟩ button to send the information to the printer.

Print Tasks

1. Click the **Print** 🖳 button on the Standard toolbar to open the Print dialog box.

2. Select the **Print Range** options of either printing **All Rows** or **Only Selected Rows**. If you choose the latter, you need to select the rows (press the ⟨⬆Shift⟩ key and click each task) before you make changes in the Print dialog box.

3. Select the **Number of Copies** and click the ⟨ OK ⟩ button to send the information to the printer.

Print Journal Entries

1. Select the journal entries you want to print and click the **Print** 🖳 button on the Standard toolbar to open the Print dialog box.

2. Select the **Print Options** if you want to **Start Each Item On a New Page** or **Print Attached Files With Item(s)**.

3. Select the **Number of Copies** and click the [OK] button to send the information to the printer.

See Also Preferences, Workspace

RECEIVE MESSAGES

The Outlook Inbox lists any new messages you receive.

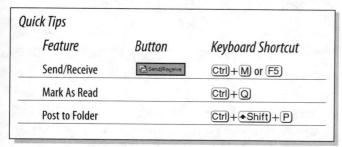

Quick Tips

Feature	Button	Keyboard Shortcut
Send/Receive	[Send/Receive]	Ctrl+M or F5
Mark As Read		Ctrl+Q
Post to Folder		Ctrl+Shift+P

Receive Messages

1. Click the **Inbox** Outlook Shortcut or the **Inbox** folder in the Folder List to view the messages you have received. You can click any of them and read the message. You can double-click the message to open it in a separate email window.

2. Click the [Send/Receive] button on the Standard toolbar to check for any new messages. If you have new messages, click the message you want to read. The body of the message is displayed in the Preview Pane. You can click in the Preview Pane and move through the message with the arrow keys and mouse pointer.

See Also Mail Delivery

REPLY TO MESSAGES

After you open and read a message, you will probably want to reply to it. You can reply to the person who sent you the message (the sender), to the sender and additional recipients, or even to a completely different set of recipients.

Quick Tips		
Feature	Button	Keyboard Shortcut
Reply	📧	Ctrl+R
Reply to All	📧	Ctrl+⬆Shift+R

Reply to a Message

1. Select the message to which you want to reply.
2. Click the **Reply** 📧 button on the Standard toolbar. Click the **Reply to All** 📧 button to send your reply to everyone included in the original message.
3. Type your reply to the message. Click the `Send ▾` button on the Standard toolbar to send the message. Notice that the message contains a reply flag and the **Subject** line contains a **RE:** to signify the message was replied to.

See Also Forward Messages, Send Messages, Receive Messages

SEARCH FOR A MESSAGE

Perhaps you received an email message that had information you need, but cannot remember which message it was in.

Quick Tips		
Feature	Button	Keyboard Shortcut
Find	🔍	Ctrl+⬆Shift+F or F3
Next Item		Ctrl+⬆Shift+> or ⬆Shift+F4
Previous Item		Ctrl+⬆Shift+<

Find a Message

1. Select the folder you want to search and click the **Find** 🖾 button on the Standard toolbar.

2. Type in the **Look For** key word(s) to find the message. Click the **Search All Text In the Message** option, otherwise the search only looks in the **From** and **Subject** areas.

3. Click the Find Now button. Click the **Close** ⊠ button when you finish using the Find feature.

TIP

If you don't find the message on your first find, you can try an advanced find. Click the **Advanced Find** Advanced Find... button in the Find message pane and narrow the scope of your find with more choices in selection criteria.

See Also Workspace

SEND MESSAGES

When you send a message online, the message is temporarily stored in the Outbox, and then it is stored in the Sent Items folder. If offline, the message stays in the Outbox until you check messages.

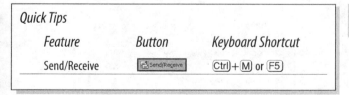

Quick Tips

Feature	*Button*	*Keyboard Shortcut*
Send/Receive	🖹 Send/Receive	Ctrl + M or F5

Send Email Messages

1. Click the 🖂 Send ▾ button on an email message and it is stored in the Outbox. If online, the message is sent immediately and a copy is stored in the Sent Items folder.

2. Click the  **Send/Receive** button on the Standard toolbar, if offline, to send the new message and check for mail. If you have your settings altered, the message may send online automatically.

See Also Mail Delivery, Receive Messages

SENT ITEMS

see Send Messages   pg 248

SIGNATURE

Outlook allows you to create an electronic *signature* or attach an electronic business card to outgoing messages.

Create a Mail Signature

1. Choose **Tools, Options; Mail Format** tab. Click the `Signature Picker...` button to open the Signature Picker dialog box.
2. Click the `New...` button to open the Create New Signature dialog box. Enter a name for your new signature in the text box and click the `Next >` button.
3. Type the information you want in the **Signature Text** and click the `Finish` button. You can click the `Edit...` button in the Signature dialog box to alter it as necessary or the `Remove` button to eliminate it.

4. Click the `OK` button to return to the Options dialog box. Make sure the new signature is selected in the

Use This Signature By Default drop-down list box
and click the ⬚ OK ⬚ button to accept changes.
Otherwise, you will have to click the Signature 📷
button and select the particular signature from the list.

TIP

If you don't want to insert the signature by default every time
you send a message, select **<None>** in the **Use This Signature
By Default** drop-down list box. When writing a message, choose
Insert, **Signature**, and select the named signature to insert for
that individual message.

See Also Mail Delivery

SORT MESSAGES

You can click the column header to toggle between sorting
on that field in ascending or descending order, or do a more
advanced column sort.

Advanced Folder Sort

Right-click the column heading (**From, Subject,
Received**) that you want to sort and choose the appropriate option from the shortcut menu.

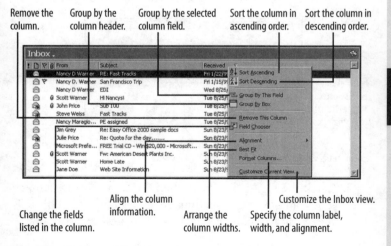

Remove the   Group by the   Group by the selected   Sort the column in   Sort the column in
column.   column header.   column field.   ascending order.   descending order.

Change the fields   Align the column   Arrange the   Specify the column label,   Customize the Inbox view.
listed in the column.   information.   column widths.   width, and alignment.

See Also Folders, Workspace

SPELLING

You can check spelling in Outlook quickly and easily. Of course, you should always review your messages for word usage errors that aren't always found by the spell checker.

Quick Tips		
Feature	*Button*	*Keyboard Shortcut*
Check Spelling	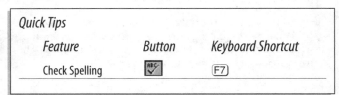	F7

Check Spelling

1. Type your message text into the body of the message window. Press the F7 key or click the **Spelling Checker** button to check spelling. Outlook highlights any misspelled words and the Spelling dialog box suggests other spellings.

2. Click the appropriate button to make the selected **Suggestions** change.

A word that shouldn't be altered.

A word that shouldn't be altered and it should not flag any other instances of the word.

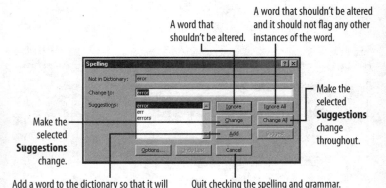

Make the selected **Suggestions** change throughout.

Make the selected **Suggestions** change.

Add a word to the dictionary so that it will remember the word as correct in the future.

Quit checking the spelling and grammar.

3. Click the ☐ OK ☐ button when Outlook displays a message telling you the spelling check is complete. This means all inaccuracies have been reviewed.

Set Spelling Options

1. Choose **Tools, Options; Spelling** tab.

2. Select the **General Options** for how your messages are checked for spelling. Click the [OK] button to accept changes.

See Also Preferences

TASKS

Creating a task list helps you organize tasks and projects significant to the dates and appointments on your schedule.

Quick Tips		
Feature	Button	Keyboard Shortcut
Create Task	☑	Ctrl + ⬆Shift + K
Create Task Request	☑	Ctrl + ⬆Shift + U

Create a Task

1. Click the **Tasks** ☑ button on the Outlook Bar. Type a new task in the **Click Here To Add a New Task** list box.

2. Click the **Due Date** drop-down arrow next to any task and select a due date for that task. Click the **Due Date** header to toggle sorting the tasks by date in ascending or descending order.

3. Click the empty check boxes to the left of any task descriptions you have recently completed. A line is drawn through the task, indicating that the task is complete.

4. Double-click a particular task to provide more detailed information in the Task window. Click the [🖫 Save and Close] button when you are finished entering information.

TIP

If you don't complete a task by a certain date, the task appears in a red font, indicating that the task wasn't completed and is past the due date.

See Also Calendar, Contacts, Journal Entries, Preferences

WORK OFFLINE

When in Outlook, you will sometimes want to work without being online. You might have some emails in your Outbox that you aren't ready to send.

Go Offline

1. Choose **File, Work Offline** to continue working in Outlook without sending or checking for email.

2. Choose **File, Work Offline** again to deselect the option and return to working online.

See Also Receive Messages, Send Messages

WORKSPACE

Outlook manages many different folders for your email and information management. Clicking the icons on the Outlook Bar can access these folders.

Quick Tips		
Feature	**Button**	**Keyboard Shortcut**
Switch to Inbox		Ctrl + ⬆Shift + I
Switch to Outbox		Ctrl + ⬆Shift + O
Move Between Calendar, TaskPad, and Folder List		Ctrl + Tab⇆ or F6
Create Office Document	🗋	Ctrl + ⬆Shift + H

View Outlook Options

1. Click the shortcut icons on the Outlook Bar to see the other options available in Outlook.

2. Click the **Outlook Shortcuts**, **My Shortcuts,** and **Other Shortcuts** groups to see the shortcut icons contained in each group.

3. Right-click the Outlook Bar and choose from the available options on the shortcut menu. You can change the icons, work with groups, and so on.

4. Click and drag a shortcut icon to drop it onto a different group to see how they can be moved.

5. Choose **View, Folder List** to see the list of Outlook folders that are available.

See Also Outlook Today, Preferences

INDEX

L

M

P